Signs, Systems, and Meanings

# Signs, Systems, and Meanings

A Contemporary Semiotic Reading

of Four Molière Plays

by Suzanne Relyea

Wesleyan
University Press
Middletown, Connecticut
1976

The Publishers gratefully acknowledge the support of the A. W. Mellon
Foundation and the Friends of Wesleyan University Press Publication
Fund toward the publication of this book.

Library of Congress Cataloging in Publication Data

Relyea, Suzanne L., 1945–
    Signs, systems, and meanings.

    Selected passages in French.
    Includes bibliographical references.
1. Molière, Jean Baptiste Poquelin, 1622–1673 — Language.
2. Semiotics.   I. Title.
PQ1866.R4             842′.4            76–8520
ISBN 0–8195–4097–8

Manufactured in the United States of America
First edition

# Contents

I wish to express my sincere appreciation to Jacques Guicharnaud for his unfailing encouragement and support from the time when this work was only a vague idea until the manuscript was accepted for publication.

I also wish to thank especially Tim Reiss and Paul De Man for their help and suggestions along the way.

— S. R.

Signs, Systems, and Meanings

# Introduction:
## Toward a Semiology of Meaning
## in Classical Theater

Recent years have witnessed the increasingly important emergence in the field of literary criticism of a pre-existing but ever-growing body of literature on the question of language and meaning. Much of this literature seems to be aimed at the discovery of precisely what constitutes meaning, or how certain systems of signs communicate to a person or group of people what we frequently call "ideas," "content," or "meaning." In France a number of modern philosophers, linguists, and critics, some of whom are called structuralists, seem, in spite of highly diversified points of view regarding specific problems, to be slowly evolving a number of similar tenets, especially in regard to the way they view the functioning of signs. The process of research and refinement in and around the problematics of verbal behavior and writing seems at present to be moving toward what is to be hoped will prove a useful definition of language in the context of a generalized science or philosophy of signs.

The question of what constitutes meaning and communication has, for some, taken the form of an investigation into the assumptions on which we base our belief in language's ability to signify. Indeed, contemporary critics are at once obsessed with and terrified by the problem of immanence and tend to be divided into two camps, according to the individual critic's convictions about the transcendental quality of the sign or the lack thereof (and, indeed, such a *lack* is always and necessarily described in negative terms — that is, in terms of absence, reappropriation, and re-presentation). Attempting to call scientific

3

discourse into play in order to write about literary language, the various structuralists tend to circumvent this problem altogether, along with that of interpretation as repetition or, in their sense, the duplication of a text. In so doing, however, they place themselves truly in the center of the problem, midway between the plenitude of scientific discourse and the immanence of literary language, so that the structuralist text itself, as a critical text, also poses the problem of meaning in terms of presence and absence. The question of a possible relationship or set of relationships between a nascent science of signs and various kinds of literary endeavor remains a difficult and crucial one.

There is a literary genre whose uniquely hybrid nature offers abundant opportunity for the simultaneous study of multiple systems of signs — of how each sign signifies and what groups of signs signify both in relation to one another and to our reading of specific texts. According to both the playwright's and the reader's historical situations, according to the notions about signs that influence them both, any one of several systems of interpretation, all of which define the critic's rhetorical and ideological framework, may emerge from such a "semiotic" reading of dramatic texts. In dealing with seventeenth-century theater, one may be tempted to allow the sign some sort of ultimate truth-value, making the signified the rational governing principle of the meaningful universe. Such an assumption, however, would indicate that the transcendent quality lent to the sign by contemporary theoretical texts must govern its nature and would result in a purely logocentric view that would give the play a somewhat biblical quality not accorded to poetic discourse in the rational *Grammars* of the period.

Without abandoning the notion of an authoritative presence in language, one may equivocate its status, as do certain seventeen-century theoretical treatises, by associating plenitude both with the Logos and with more human logoi: consciousness, intellect, feelings, inner experience, and so on. This latter option seems to be implicit in seventeenth-century rationalism. Meaning is a represented entity both human and divine. It is definable as the *cogito*, and its ontological status need not be called into question. Representation is an imitation of that ambiguous entity apparently internal to language, yet whose existence is nevertheless guaranteed from outside the sign itself. Meaning cannot be restored to view on the printed page except by God, but can be faithfully represented by the God-given (i.e. "natural") device of

4

sound[1] and transcribed into writing. The text of the play thus becomes a simple mnemotechnic device allowing actors to represent the real entity, the meaning of the play. The production "produces" or *brings forward* meaning, the immediacy of which we can perceive, while the text remains decidedly deficient in this capacity. Like a page of music, it "means" only to the extent that it indicates a performance.

In a theatrical production or, more specifically, representation — since the seventeenth century concerned itself more with a theory of representation than with an analysis of meaning in the modern sense — perceivable verbal and bodily gestures created by the actors, and the systems of signs constituted by those gestures, add another complex dimension to the communication which transpires. Since my concern is with seventeenth-century drama, I have not in any sense attempted to delineate a semiology of communication or typology of theatrical gesture, as, for example, the science of kinesics attempts to analyze body motion using linguistic catagories. While such an endeavor seems highly desirable for a generalized science of signs, signals, and symbols, it is highly doubtful that sufficient data about the various contemporary productions of Molière's plays is available for the reading of specific texts to be facilitated in any way. However, insofar as the question of gesture is inseparable from that of meaning on stage, and insofar as the young Molière was trained in mime, such considerations cannot be excluded from a reading of his texts that would include both seventeenth-century and twentieth-century commentary on signs, representation, and meaning.

"Meaning as presence" implies the corollary "gesture as illustration." While modern critics continue to confront the iron-clad tradition which views semiotic praxis as an illustration, duplication, or representation of the word-presence,[2] in the context of seventeenth-century rationalism, gesture remains a purely accessory and essentially barbaric system of symbols. Similarly, theater historians have tended to view ancient Greek beast mummeries and mimes as contributing to the "origins" of the development of "real," "modern" comedy, that is, as crude or rudimentary forms of the genre of which Aristophanes is generally considered the first master. Consider the following hypothetical reconstruction of the history of comedy:

> In Attica, the universal folk-mummery took the form of an animal masquerade attached as *comos* to the worship

of Dionysus as god of the vinous revel. Their phallic procession sang lampoons against chance bystanders, sometimes more elaborately against public characters. At first their performance, or at any rate their remarks were impromptu; later a poet wrote lines for them. When the poet's work attained some elaboration, he wrote an address for the chorus to sing before they withdrew. Next an actor was introduced, partly because the Megarian farce was becoming popular. He was attired in the Peloponnesian manner, and his part was at first mere clowning with the chorus after the parabasis. Later he invaded the earlier part of the performance and was in time provided with a colleague, so that genuine dramatic action became possible.[3]

The implication is clearly one of progress viewed as the refining of crude, disorganized practices, and assumes a necessary association between the existence of modern comedy, defined as *"genuine* dramatic action," and a written text. Indeed, the essential intervention facilitating this progress is that of the poet-author, and the essential couple whose existence certifies the authenticity of dramatic action is that of poet and actor — "âge du livre" in the history of literature, period in the history of thought to which Molière and, more importantly, modern literary criticism also belong.

Similarly, Molière critics have to a large extent avoided his apprenticeship in mime except to mention it as a contributing factor in the evolution of his writing, in somewhat the same way as Gilbert Norwood views the beast mummeries. One thus often finds the farces implicitly or explicitly reduced to the status of a developmental stage, albeit a necessary and marginally interesting one, in the poet-author's evolution toward the writing of "high" comedy:

> Mais la diversité même des tendances pouvait embarrasser un débutant, si doué fût-il. Molière procède aux essais et options nécessaires en bénéficiant des efforts contemporarains, tout en affermissant par une progression très calculée sa propre originalité. Encore ne franchira-t-il que prudemment les étapes.
>
> C'est par de simples farces qu'il commence, très tôt, sa carrière d'auteur. Il y excellait comme acteur, et ces courtes fantaisies, lestement jouées, en contraste

6

plaisant avec les œuvres plus soutenues, contribuaient pour une large part à la réputation de la troupe. Elles pouvaient se réduire à des pochades, sinon à des canevas qui donnaient toute liberté à l'improvisation: la mimique et les jeux de scène restaient l'essentiel, conformément à la tradition de la "commedia dell'arte" et souvent encore de la comédie italienne. Mais il lui était aisé d'étoffer à son gré ces "divertissements" pour les élever au rang de "petites comédies," selon les termes dont il les qualifiera plus tard.[4]

I have undertaken to demonstrate that this critical attitude is not without relation to an ideology of signs implicit in French classical drama and explicitly commented upon in the Port-Royal *Grammar* and then in the *Logic*. As I see most clearly in *L'Ecole des femmes*, a hierarchical distribution of signs and of various semiotic systems indeed functions and is even thematized in Molière's works. However, it seems to me a mistake to imitate that hierarchical distribution in twentieth-century critical discourse simply in order to comment on it. The semiology of meaning toward which I wish to work, while I do not hold it to be that scientific discourse to which semiologies of communication often aspire, may serve to point out just those areas of critical blindness in a rhetoric whose chief aim is to render large chunks of time preparatory, thus valorizing a given moment, past or present.

In the *Cours de linguistique générale*, Saussure, who, as Jacques Derrida points out, is not always entirely free of a fundamentally Cartesian view of being and signifying in language,[5] also considers spoken verbal language a more advanced "cultural convention" than the primitive "natural" system of gesture; "langage" is natural to man, but not "langue." Only the faculty for, or possibility of, the constitution of a language ("un système de signes distincts, correspondant à des idées distinctes")[6] is natural. Ideas are natural; systems of signs, cultural. But some systems of signs are more cultural than others:

Ainsi pour Whitney, qui assimile la langue à une institution sociale au même titre que toutes les autres, c'est par hasard, pour de simples raisons de commodité, que nous nous servons de l'appareil vocal comme instrument de la langue: les hommes auraient pu aussi bien choisir le geste et employer des images visuelles au lieu d'images acoustiques. Sans doute cette thèse est trop absolue; la langue n'est pas une institution sociale en tous points semblable aux autres; de plus, Whitney va trop loin quand il dit que notre choix est tombé par hasard sur les organes vocaux; ils nous étaient bien imposés par la nature. Mais sur le point essentiel, le linguiste américain nous semble avoir raison: la langue est une convention, et la nature du signe dont on est convenu est indifférente.[7]

The vocal apparatus is a more natural, and therefore a more suitable, instrument for the production and exchange of signs than those parts of the body which produce gesture. Yet the evolved system of signs, the convention ("langue") is highly valorized as a social institution unlike others, and continues to be so throughout Saussure's *Cours*. The tension between nature and culture so frequent in the work of ethnologists and found here in Saussure, as well as in the work of many other modern linguists, provides the bias from which most critics implicitly or explicitly interpret the somewhat ambiguous status of gesture as a system of signs in Western literature. However, such is not my own purpose; rather, I would stress the relationship between this nature / culture duality and the couple "langue" / "langage." The latter seems to correspond to a differentiation between the general and the particular, or, more precisely, between virtuality and actuality:

> Pris dans son tout, le langage est multiforme et hétéroclite; à cheval sur plusieurs domaines, à la fois physique, physiologique et psychique, il appartient encore au domaine social; il ne se laisse classer dans aucune catégorie des faits humains, parce qu'on ne sait comment dégager son unité.[8]

> La langue, au contraire, est un tout en soi et un principe de classification. Dès que nous lui donnons la première place parmi les faits de langage, nous introduisons un ordre natural dans un ensemble qui ne se prête à aucune autre classification.[9]

The image is of a form, the only possible one, given to a disturbingly amorphous mass. This mass, precisely because it does not correspond to the "content" or "spirit" half of the Cartesian principle, represents an important modification in the course of the writing of the story of meaning. It marks that moment at which language ceases to describe itself entirely in terms of metaphysical categories, that moment at which one may begin to recognize the inadequacy of those categories for such description.

The *Cours de linguistique générale,* as a moment of transition, suspends its author in a no-man's land between two ways of talking about the problem of meaning, between an established tradition of categories of being and a nascent one: the use of categories of language qua language, which are not reducible to metaphysics. I as a reader of Molière find myself on similarly ambiguous terrain. Although generally lacking any faith in the adequacy of metaphysical categories to locate and describe meaning, including that vocabulary of origin and development which arranges and valorizes ways of using signs hierarchically, we of the present are nonetheless faced with texts which reflect a belief in that adequacy. In other words, one is faced with a notion of language prevalent in seventeenth-century epistemology, grammar, logic, and psychology, in Descartes' physics and metaphysics, and in that ensemble of objective ideas and principles which came to be known, in the second half of the century, as "Cartesianism."

Now Cartesianism defines language as a tool for and an element in the search for the foundations and methods of science and metaphysics. It constructs a theory of representation in terms of the self, the world, and God. It obeys the laws governing the two substances, matter and spirit, with all the subtleties implicit in the relation of the spatial distribution of signs to the thoughts which that distribution purportedly portrays. Such a notion has as a corollary the authoritative truth value of a signified whose relation to the signifier remains as clear and intelligible as the link between the *sum* and the *cogito* is often mistakenly assumed to be. *Significans ergo significatus,* the fundamental intuition being that in order to signify, I must signify something which could not be signified if it, and I, and ultimately God, did not exist. Indeed, while the bond between signifier and signified is never questioned, the nature of the latter seems wholly equivocal. In the second half of the seventeenth century the signified appears to take on the quality of a paradoxically interiorized (into the sign), extratextual referent. In modern terms it is precisely that mystify-

9

ing appropriation by the intrinsic immanent universe of the text of the extrinsic transcendant world of Truth and experience that lends authoritative presence to the sign and truth-value to the "content" of both Molière's and René Jasinski's texts.

As Noam Chomsky points out in his study *Cartesian Linguistics,*

> . . . Descartes himself devoted little attention to language and his few remarks are subject to various interpretations . . . Still it seems to me that there is, in the period under review here, a coherent and fruitful development of a body of ideas and conclusions regarding the nature of language in association with a certain theory of mind and that this development can be regarded as an outgrowth of the Cartesian revolution.[10]

In a note he adds, "It should be borne in mind that we are dealing with a period that antedates the divergence of linguistics, philosophy, and psychology."[11] Similarly, I shall frequently have to invoke the body of theory contained in the Port-Royal *Grammar* and *Logic*, as well as the basic tenets of Cartesian rationalism in order to identify the underlying assumptions governing Molière's characters' use of physical and verbal signs. The whole constellation of ideas and assumptions stemming from "Cartesianism" and, more directly, from the Port-Royal texts reappears continually in the tradition of philosophical grammar which developed from that Port-Royal *Grammar*. It therefore constitutes the historical perspective of my work. My point of view, my own discourse, however, remains that of someone writing at a time when linguistics, philosophy, and psychology do indeed consider themselves separate disciplines, and when the Cartesian faith — in a movement that continually surpasses itself, a progression from finite to Infinite via doubt, the *cogito*, and several proofs of the existence of God — has been replaced by an analysis or science of signs strictly contained within language itself.

In my attempt to identify semiotic systems and ways of functioning within and without them in seventeenth-century comedy, I shall be speaking principally about Arnolphe and Agnès in *L'Ecole des femmes*, Tartuffe and Orgon in *Tartuffe*, Dom Juan and Sganarelle in *Dom Juan*, and Jupiter, Amphitryon, Mercury, and Sosie in *Amphitryon*. It should be clearly noted that it is neither my desire nor my intention to offer a complete analysis of the plays involved. Instead, with these characters, I wish to identify the elements of a specific semiology of meaning inseparable from a continued meditation in Molière's works on a personal, social, and aesthetic dilemma that was surely quite poignant for him, especially in the historical context in question.

All of the above characters are either very concerned about rhetorical skills and the relationship between what is said and what is meant, or cause others to be so concerned or both, as in the cases of Arnolphe and Tartuffe. Taking the plays in chronological order, from *L'Ecole des femmes* to *Dom Juan*, there is clearly a refinement of effective speaking ability which is undone in *Amphitryon* by a confusion of identities. Indeed, rhetorical skill is characterized by the manipulation of signs regardless of their generally accepted signified, or by an illicit modification of the relationship between the two. We reach a point where language becomes an opaque screen either purposefully blocking any communication whatsoever or communicating what it does not say in an entirely ironic mode. Effective speaking ability therefore constitutes a knotty moral dilemma because of the considerable and most often dangerous power it affords the speaker. His increasing proficiency and accompanying tendency to dissociate signifier and signified, or the subversion of the bond between the two, are invariably aimed at some illicit personal gain, the attainment of which would endanger the very existence of the significant nucleus around which the play is structured (family, *salon*, court, society at large, Heaven itself). Speech, like the play and like language itself,[12] is made up of signs and can be destroyed by them if one member of the linguistic community does not obey the generally accepted rules of exchange. Insofar as Tartuffe and Dom Juan are concerned, the problem of conveying meaning is entirely synonymous with that of telling the truth or of keeping one's word, and both find themselves pressured into doing one or both of these. For Sosie, saying what one means and meaning what one says are bound up with the problem of identity and subjectivity, the implication being that there is no meaning without a clearly defined subject, for it is the latter who creates significance in a kind of Cartesian ontological proof of the existence of Meaning.

# Classical *Sēmē*
# and Classical *Epistēmē*

... jamais cependant jusqu'à ce jour on n'a pu ob-
server qu'aucun animal en soit venu à ce point de
perfection d'user d'un véritable langage, c'est-à-dire,
d'exprimer ... quelque chose qui puisse se rapporter
à la seule pensée et non à l'impulsion naturelle.
— Descartes,
Letter to Morus, 1649[1]

Il nous reste à examiner ce qu'elle [la parole] a de
spirituel, qui fait l'un des plus grands avantages de
l'homme au-dessus de tous les autres animaux et qui
est une des plus grandes preuves de la raison.
— *La Grammaire générale et
raisonnée de Port-Royal*[2]

... le discours n'est pas simplement ce qui traduit
les luttes ou les systèmes de domination, mais ce
pour quoi, ce par quoi on lutte, le pouvoir dont on
cherche à s'emparer.
— Michel Foucault[3]

Molière was certainly not a rationalist. Hardly a devotee of Descartes or of the various rationalist philosophies already blossom-
ing in the second half of the seventeenth century,[4] his theater
depends in large part on those elements of experience about
which Descartes was most skeptical: bodies, forms, colors, and
gestures, all eminently theatrical elements, especially characteris-
tic of the farce, to which he in part remained faithful throughout
his career.[5] Recreating nature with his own language, forms,
textures, and colors, he asks us to believe in surfaces, in the exteriority of bodies, gestures, and set design, and in the situations
they produce. This world of sensual artifice, of stereotypical or
prototypical characters, of created tones, distances, substances,

and light — and our acceptance of it — constitute the specifically theatrical aspect of the audience's listening and viewing experience. Theatricality, and comedy in particular, would appear the very antithesis of the fundamental Cartesian suspicion concerning the senses and their relationship to reality. In Descartes' works, chronologically, the study of physics precedes that of metaphysics, the latter actually growing out of a reaction to the former. The famous tree analogy that appears in the letter-preface of the *Principles of Philosophy* depicts metaphysics as roots, physics as the trunk, and medicine, mechanics, and morals as the branches of a coherent system.[6] The *Meditations* also presuppose the chronological anteriority of science. Their search for certitude begins with a total doubt that assumes belief in the very objectivity it proceeds to negate and surpass. The chronological progression via the *cogito* moves from objects to the self to God, but God constitutes a *sine qua non* as the creator of the self and of objects.

There is thus a clear distinction between the epistemological and ontological levels of Descartes' work; and the truth of his thought, his method, and his science can be certified only at the highest ontological level. The third Meditation makes it clear that while ideas, or images (representations) of things to the self, emotions and desires, cannot in and of themselves be false, we can and do err in our judgments. In judging, "je conçois bien alors quelque chose comme le sujet de l'action de mon esprit, mais j'ajoute aussi quelque autre chose par cette action à l'idée que j'ai de cette chose-là."[7] Judgments consist of two kinds of implicit affirmations: first, that our idea resembles a thing, and secondly, that that thing really exists outside of the self. This is precisely the problem:

> Or la principale erreur . . . consiste en ce que je juge que les idées qui sont en moi sont semblables ou conformes à des choses qui sont hors de moi; car certainement si je considérais seulement les idées comme de certains modes ou façons de ma pensée, sans les vouloir rapporter à quelque chose d'extérieur, à peine me pourraient-elles donner occasion de faillir.[8]

The refutation in Meditations I and II of any necessary resemblance between perception and thing, and even of the existence of things, leads to a similar doubt about the similarity between idea and thing — that is, about language. Judging implies a subject, a verb, and an attribute; this last is that which my mind adds to the idea I have of something, and so, like that idea, it does not necessarily have any ontological value.

There is, however, one exception, one moment at which I can glimpse the certitude that my idea corresponds to objective reality and my language to truth. That moment concerns my intuition about the existence of the Infinite, the only possible guarantee of my language.

> . . . il faut nécessairement conclure . . . que Dieu existe, car encore que l'idée de la substance soit en moi de cela même que je suis une substance, je n'aurais pas néanmoins l'idée d'une substance infinie, moi qui suis un être fini, si elle n'avait été mise en moi par quelque substance qui fut véritablement infinie.[9]

> Cette idée, dis-je, d'un être souverainement parfait et infini est très vraie; car encore que peut-être l'on puisse feindre qu'un tel être n'existe point, on ne peut pas feindre néanmoins que son idée ne me représente rien de réel.[10]

Descartes' working progression from the world to Being (and the all-encompassing doubt he strives to maintain at the level of the human mind and of the real world) seems very far from the game of illusion and false resemblances on which Molière's theater depends. The fact that Descartes' and Molière's works are, from this point of view, the very antithesis of one another suggests, however, some kind of dialectical relationship. Indeed, one of the goals of the present work is to point out the relationship between the way in which Molière's characters use and abuse language and a hierarchical philosophy of mind whose end is certitude in the Creator and which distinguishes men from beasts according to the presence or absence of thought and language. Together with the Port-Royal *Grammar* and *Logic*, Descartes' works imply and sometimes state a view of words as vehicles for the expression of thought, invented by men solely for that purpose. The letter quoted above from Descartes to Henry More continues: "Ce langage est en effet le seul signe certain d'une pensée latente dans le corps; tous les hommes en usent . . . mais aucune bête ne peut en user; c'est pourquoi il est permis de prendre le langage pour la vraie différence entre les hommes et les bêtes."[11]

This attitude pervades all of Descartes' work and seems to have deeply influenced his pupil and sometimes adversary, Antoine Arnauld, coauthor of the Port-Royal *Grammar* and of the *Logic*, both of which are partially inspired by Cartesian philosophy.[12] Much of the comedy in Molière's plays depends upon the emotion and concentrated dramatic energy flowing from, between, and among the characters and situations he creates. Generally speaking, the funnier the scene, the less clear and intelligent the comic character's thoughts, and the more evident his feelings about the situation. Harpagon's hysterical monologue upon discovering the theft of his money is an archetypal example. The farcelike physical and verbal gestures in this and many similar scenes correlate with a notion of bestiality (with considerable stress on the presence of an idea of lower *phyla*) based on elements of confusion and inarticulation.[13] Such a lack of control is most typical of those who lose in Molière. The winners usually maintain linguistic and intellectual domination over the other characters and quickly become losers if that domination slips away. In Act III, scene ii, of *L'Ecole des femmes*, Arnolphe, being his most confident, tyrannical, and controlling self, orders an apparently submissive, suffering Agnès to read the "Maximes du mariage." Chauveau's illustration for the 1666 edition of the play shows him pointing to the center of his forehead as he says, "Là, regardez-moi là, durant cet entretien" (line 677). It is as though the content of his brain, which Agnès is to contemplate, given the form of his language, to which she is to listen attentively, constitutes the source of his power, which for the moment remains quite unshaken. In the last scene of the play, broken and defeated, "s'en allant tout transporté, et ne pouvant parler,"[14] as Molière comments, Arnolphe can only exclaim "Ouf." Linguistically speaking, he exits on all fours.

If there is anything striking about Arnolphe, it is certainly the amount of talking he does. Dominating the stage with his black and green — a trifle overgreen — presence,[15] he opens and closes numerous scenes and entire acts with his long monologues. His discourse is so voluminous that one has the impression he must resent everyone else's lines, their very capacity for language, or, in Cartesian terms, their capacity for thought and hence for humanity. It is very clear that he resents this capacity insofar as Agnès is concerned, and, as a matter of fact, Agnès *is* his slave, since he bought her when she was four. It is therefore not surprising, even to the generous and liberal Chrysalde, that he not treat her entirely as a person, for such are the times. What does surprise Arnolphe's friend, however, are the marriage plans in the rather immediate offing. He cannot help remarking: "Prendre femme est à vous un coup bien téméraire" (I. i. 8), alluding to Arnolphe's forty-two years. "Only because," replies Arnolphe,

> . . . votre front, je crois, veut que du mariage
> Les cornes soient partout l'infaillible apanage. [I. i. 11–12]

Arnolphe, one of Molière's several stereotypical representatives of a certain nascent middle class, and the most possessive of men, not only wants to own Agnès, but plans to be the unique proprietor of logical discourse, the omniscient silencer of passionate exchange, and thus the unique proprietor of honorable and happy marriage. No city houses as many patient, forgiving, and stupid husbands as his own, he feels, but he possesses the secret to immunity. In a manner typical of his class in Molière's works, he describes the situation, or rather his own obsession, in grotesquely monetary terms. Some unfaithful wives (for they are all unfaithful) shower their lovers with the cuckold's hard-earned money. Others amass gifts explained away as the rewards of pristine virtue. Still others delight their spouses with sums of money won at the gaming tables, while the latter studiously avoid the question "What game?" As for Arnolphe's place in this tableau:

> . . . ce sont partout des sujets de satire,
> Et comme spectateur ne puis-je pas en rire? [I. i. 43–44]

After all, he painted it. His election of a spectator role thus remains inseparable from his dual preoccupation with conquest and acquisition, that is, with acquisition as a means of rising above and dominating ordinary men, which is to say everyone else. In Bernard Magné's terms, the struggle in which both he and Agnès are engaged, albeit in opposite directions, may be represented by the homology DISCOURSE = KNOWLEDGE = POWER, and the inverse proportion of the length of Agnès's speeches to the importance of Arnolphe's monologues by the following diagram:[16]

| Acts | Monologues by Arnolphe | Speeches by Agnès | |
|------|------------------------|-------------------|---|
| I | 22 lines | 4 lines, of which the first: "Oui Monsieur, Dieu merci." CONSENTEMENT ET SOUMISSION | DISCOURS SOUMIS |
| II | 27 lines | 100 lines | DISCOURS NAÏF |
| III | 67 lines | Maximes | DISCOURS ALIÉNÉ |
| | | ——[nocturnal rendez-vous] | |
| IV | 80 lines | 0 lines (absence) | SILENCE |
| | | ——[kidnapping]—— | |
| V | 8 lines | 50 lines of which the last: "Je *veux* rester ici." RÉSISTANCE ET VOLONTÉ | DISCOURS INDÉPENDANT |

However, Chrysalde also plays a considerable role in the struggle to either monopolize with monologue or to institute genuine dialogue (i.e. exchange); for twenty-five lines, and with some difficulty, he has been trying to say something, and finally succeeds in holding the floor for another twenty-eight. The two friends have henceforth, and for the duration of the scene, locked horns (no pun intended). For the moment the struggle does not directly involve Agnès, but rather a reciprocal desire to appropriate discourse. Chrysalde claims to speak with authority and clearly feels that his interlocutor should therefore listen and acquiesce:

J'entends parler le monde; et des gens se délassent
A venir débiter les choses qui se passent [I. i. 47–48]

Thiş is neither the first nor the last time a Molière character has used the authority of "le monde" to force another to accept his opinion or do his bidding; in *Le Misanthrope* Arsinoé uses the same device with Célimène, but to no avail. "I don't like cuck-oldry either," says Chrysalde:

> Pourtant je n'ai jamais affecté de le dire;
> Car enfin il faut craindre un revers de satire. [I. i. 55–56]

Proclamation, like knowledge, renders vulnerable at the same time as it accords power, and Chrysalde would like to point out that Arnolphe is running a risk both in marrying Agnès and in preaching his marry-an-imbecile doctrine. (Significantly, Chrys-alde's next three speeches will consist of one line apiece.) How-ever that may be, his long speech does represent an attempt to convey to Arnolphe his own thoughts about cuckoldry, as well as about language — that is, to teach him something — and such is precisely the kind of receptivity Arnolphe most studiously avoids. Obsessed with a single and singular (monogamous-monologos) thought, escape from cuckoldry — and the attainment thereby of a higher plane of existence — he necessarily wishes not to deal with other peoples' thoughts and language. At the extreme, in his relationship with Agnès, he insists on the total vacuousness which alone allows his hunger for monologue to approach satiation:

> . . . c'est assez pour elle, à vous en bien parler,
> De savoir prier Dieu, m'aimer, coudre et filer. [I. i. 101–02]

The same kind of dynamic comes into play with Chrysalde, although somewhat less aggressively, since he cannot easily de-prive a friend and equal who has similar concerns about mono-logue and monopolization of his human capacity, as he wishes to do to Agnès, but he can remain totally immune to the other's words and thus to his knowledge and thoughts.

> Vous serez ébahi quand vous serez au bout,
> Que vous ne m'aurez rien persuadé du tout. [I. i. 121–22]

Arnolphe seems as certain of being right as Descartes was that only God is certainly right. The doctrine of divine truth, which in the *Meditations* forms so integral a part of Descartes' reflection on man's relationship to God, establishes the fact that, although limited, our understanding knows unerringly what it truly knows: "D'où est-ce donc que naissent mes erreurs? C'est à savoir, de cela seul que, la volonté étant beaucoup plus ample et plus étendue que l'entendement, je ne la contiens pas dans les mêmes limites, mais que je l'étends aussi aux choses que je n'entends pas."[17] Will, along with words, is that of which Arnolphe seems to exhibit the greatest quantity. Descartes may have a method — everyone does, declares Arnolphe — but "En femme, comme en tout, je veux suivre ma mode" (I. i. 124). A foreshadowing of Dom Juan, the incorrigible autonomy-seeker, the seducer who cannot be seduced? Surely, but more appropriately here, a portrait of an aging bourgeois who pours forth a copious current of ambitious desire from a rather slim intellectual source. And desire, as will become increasingly evident in my discussion of *Tartuffe* and *Dom Juan*, dangerously disrupts the clarity and order of any system of signs: ". . . il est, en l'homme, des puissances de brouillage qui jouent à la jointure du langage et de la pensée pour compromettre le fonctionnement naturel et rationnel du modèle représentatif et qui ont nom, amour-propre, concupiscence, cupidité, désir."[18]

Anticipating Chrysalde's question, Arnolphe explains:

> Pourquoi cette narration?
> C'est pour vous rendre instruit de ma précaution. [I. i. 149–50]

He thinks very little, in fact modestly limits himself to an *idée fixe*, rudely rejects his friend's input in order not to complicate things, judges a great deal, and, sometimes assuming a pedagogical role, attempts to impose his judgments on others (Agnès and, to a lesser extent, Chrysalde). It is altogether apropos that at the end of the scene, having asked Chrysalde for a judgment about Agnès, he tells him in advance what it will be:

> Vous pourrez, dans cette conférence,
> Juger de sa personne et de son innocence. [I. i. 155–56]

The intervention of the notion of judgment at this point in the play is crucial to our understanding of Arnolphe and of the theory of knowledge reflected in *L'Ecole dés femmes* in general. Its ontological and grammatical value are both clearly defined in the seventeenth century. In the third Meditation, Descartes places that notion in the context of the categorization of different kinds of thoughts. Of these there are three: ideas, or "images of things," "comme lorsque je me représente un homme, ou une chimère, ou le ciel, ou un ange, ou Dieu même"; desires or emotions ("volontés ou affections"), "comme lorsque je veux, que je crains"; and, lastly, judgments, "comme lorsque . . . j'affirme

ou que je nie."[19] In the second and third cases, "je conçois bien
. . . quelque chose comme le sujet de l'action de mon esprit,
mais j'ajoute aussi quelque autre chose par cette action à l'idée
que j'ai de cette chose-là."[20] The presence of a subject-concept
(I, a man, a fantasy, the sky, an angel, or God) is clearly implied,
but the thinker acts upon that concept, adding something to it.
To the subject, a verb is joined; to the noun, grammar and syntax. Judgments are specifically distinguished as those thoughts
in which we may and most often do err. Whether a concept we
imagine corresponds to experiential reality or not, we nevertheless
conceive of it; therefore it cannot be false, properly speaking. In
the same way, whether I desire or feel something bad, or even
nonexistent, it nevertheless is true that I desire or feel it. However, everything I affirm or negate can be either true or false.

The Port-Royal *Grammar*, inspired both by the "bon usage"
doctrine and by Cartesian rationalism, takes up Descartes' definition, but in grammatical terms: ". . . les hommes ne parlent
guère pour exprimer simplement ce qu'ils conçoivent; mais c'est
presque toujours pour exprimer les jugements qu'ils font des
choses qu'ils conçoivent."[21] This statement introduces the discussion of judgments in Part II, chapter 1, entitled "Que la
connaissance de ce qui se passe dans notre esprit est nécessaire
pour comprendre les fondements de la Grammaire; et que c'est
de là que dépend la diversité des mots qui composent le discours."[22] Part II of the *Grammar* is in fact devoted to an analysis
of the way in which signs mean, and it is in this context, and in
that of grammatical structures as faithful reflections of the structures of the mind, that we must consider the discussion of
judgments.

> Le jugement que nous faisons des choses, comme quand
> je dis, "la terre est ronde," s'appelle PROPOSITION; et
> ainsi toute proposition enferme nécessairement deux
> termes: l'un appelé "sujet," qui est ce dont on affirme,
> comme "terre"; et l'autre appelé "attribut," qui est ce
> qu'on affirme, comme "ronde": et de plus la liaison entre
> ces deux termes, "est."[23]

Statements, or judgments, are composed of two kinds of words:
those that signify the objects of our thoughts and those that
signify the putting into form of thoughts. The first are originally
autonomous concepts molded into the material terms of judgments, the subject and attribute. In this group are included

nouns, articles, pronouns, participles, prepositions, and adverbs. The rest of the words in a sentence are "la forme et la manière de nos pensées," or the act by which we affirm the attribute of the subject. In this second group are included only verbs, conjunctions, and interjections.

Within the context of this strictly bipolar notion of language, wherein body and mind find grammatical echoes in concepts and verbs, Arnolphe speaks almost entirely from the verbal, or willful, side of the dichotomy, and his judgments are thus doomed to error. Just as Descartes makes it clear that neither half of the duality has any essential or ontological value except as part of the whole, so the Port-Royal grammarians indicate that a sentence can have meaning only when it contains both concepts and action upon them; the *Logic*, published two years after the *Grammar*, applies the doctrine of the latter to the art of thinking, proposing itself as a tonic against defective judgments, that is, judgments which do not reflect reality. In both works, meaning, at the level of the sentence, seems to be a function of an interspace, of the interaction between ideas and verbs, and therein, precisely, lies much of the comedy of Arnolphe's discourse. He errs in his judgments with such consistency that he resembles a counter illustration of the *Logic*, the artless thinker par excellence. To be sure, he uses subjects, verbs, and attributes, but whereas the Port-Royal bipolar division of the parts of speech demonstrates that quantity lies with the concept-linked words, Arnolphe's lines are particularly rich in verbs and just as poor in ideas.

Act I, scene iii, Arnolphe's first interview with Agnès, grammatically demonstrates the opposition of nis verb-laden, imperative attitude toward her to the pseudo-aggressive manner in which he speaks of the world outside his home-fortress:

> Allez, montez là-haut:
> Ne vous ennuyez point, je reviendrai tantôt,
> Et je vous parlerai d'affaires importantes.

> (tous étant rentrés)

> Héroines du temps, Mesdames les savantes,
> Pousseuses de tendresse et de beaux sentimens,
> Je défie à la fois tous vos vers, vos romans,
> Vos lettres, billets doux, toute votre science
> De valoir cette honnête et pudique ignorance. [I. iii. 241 ff.]

21

It is striking that while the first two and a half alexandrines contain five verbs, in the following five there is only one conjugated verb whose "challenge" is smothered in a heap of nouns and adjectives, thus turning into a kind of comic irony by reversal.

The bravado with which Arnolphe throws out his claim of victory over a chaotic, cuckoldry-ridden outside world in fact parallels his terror of the complexities of a language alien to him and over which he can maintain no control. His view of the "beau monde" would seem as obsessive as his attitude toward Agnès; nicely expressed feelings, poems, novelettes, love letters, and generally knowledgeable women are all treacherous by their very nature, less because of what they do than because of their talent for metaphor, a talent sadly deficient in Arnolphe's own love speech (V. 4). What he most fears and needs to conquer in the protective interiority of his home, and of his carefully constructed and controlled relationship with Agnès, is that capacity by which his century defines humanity — that is language use — and a literal or full language at that. I shall have more to say about the relationship between that language and the semiological value of systems of objects in an enclosed living space in my discussion of Tartuffe's confiscation of Orgon's house. For the moment, let us examine more closely its relation to the contemporary concepts of representation, knowledge, and judgment.

In his book *Cartesian Linguistics* Noam Chomsky summarizes the seventeenth-century proof of humanity by language:

> In short, then, man has a species-specific capacity, a unique type of intellectual organization which cannot be attributed to peripheral organs or related to general intelligence and which manifests itself in what we may refer to as the "creative aspect" of ordinary language use — its property being both unbounded in scope and stimulus-free. . . . Thus Descartes maintains that language is available for the free expression of thought or for appropriate response in any new context and is undetermined by any fixed association of utterances to external stimuli or physiological states.[24]

Arnolphe's plan is to limit Agnès's discourse to his own understanding of it and then to dominate it with monologue; to thus restrict her to the recording of immediate sensory perceptions is to prevent her, in Port-Royal terms, from making any sort of judgment whatsoever. He would have her remain at the level of the concept or idea. Ideas, however, in both Descartes' and Arnauld's works, are simply things as presented to the mind; there is no guarantee of their existence in the objective world, so that the truth which they possess by definition is hardly dependent on any such correspondence. They may be more or less clear because of the censoring or modification brought about by inattention, prejudice, or misleading expression, but these defects do not effect the truth-value of the idea and can be cleared away by a closer scrutiny of the conceiver's state of mind.[25] As we have seen, the relationship between the idea and reality, and thus the possibility of error, intervenes in the process of judgment.[26] Thus in seventeenth-century epistemological terms, Arnolphe seeks to judge for Agnès, to mediate between her and the world and so to be her will, her arbiter, in a discourse in which things and words cease to coincide for Agnès and can only be reunited in the semiology of her exchanges with Horace (whence the tremendous significance of her missive-missile to him). Admittedly, Arnolphe possesses will enough for two, but his readiness to share does not in this case sufficiently counterbalance the moral implications of depriving Agnès of her freedom to engage in dialogue, of the discovery of her very identity. He would suppress that "species-specific capacity" defined by Chomsky as the "creative aspect of ordinary language use — its property being both unbounded in scope and stimulus-free." In seeking to limit her responses to external stimuli which he can carefully control, and in administering a grotesquely farcesque "speak-only-when-spoken-to" linguistic doctrine, he effectively problematizes her humanity for a time in the play (see Magné's chart, above, and especially the secret "off stage" notations between Acts III and IV, and IV and V).

Molière reminds us early on that such a horrendously tyrannical project is doomed to failure. Enter Horace, bringing with him the possibility of a comic convention dating at least from Menander: a beautiful young slave girl spirited away from a libidinous, repulsive old fogy by a dashing young male lead. Molière elaborates on the traditional scheme, lending such intricacy to its pattern that the comedy of *L'Ecole des femmes* emerges as commentary on universal patterns of exchange, to the conspicuous exclusion of money. Whereas the exceedingly handsome but not terribly clever young man of the convention is generally seconded by a compensatingly astute slave, Horace, through no effort of his own, is seconded by the would-be master, himself in a scramble for a woman, for words in dialogue, and finally for the liberation of personal identity which would facilitate that dialogue. The key is of course a confusion of identities which can be traced to and will be dissipated by Oronte and Enrique. The letter from his father to Arnolphe which Horace faithfully delivers during his first encounter with the latter (I. iv) sows the seeds of a dénouement that might otherwise appear entirely unwarranted and indeed remains incongruous to some critics.[27] In this same scene Arnolphe advises Horace of the ease with which a young "gaillard" can give horns to the husbands of his city:

> . . . pour ceux que du nom de galans on baptise,
> Ils ont en ce pays de quoi se contenter,
> Car les femmes y sont faites à coqueter:
> On trouve d'humeur douce et la brune et la blonde,
> Et les maris aussi les plus bénins du monde [I. iv. 293 ff.]

The irony resides in the allusion to "baptism," which, by its very conventional nature, cleverly conceals and suggests the secret of the dénouement. Arnolphe and Horace do not know who each other are insofar as their competition for Agnès is concerned, and neither knows who Agnès is by birth, as she herself remains ignorant of her origin. Arnolphe is just reiterating to Horace what he has been telling us all along, that the women are easy and the husbands stupid, but the author behind him inscribes double and triple meaning into his every word.

Unaware that he is setting himself up to become a cuckold, Arnolphe urges Horace on:

> Les gens faits comme vous font plus que les écus,
> Et vous êtes de taille à faire des cocus. [I. iv. 301–02]

He may strive to monopolize knowledge by monologue, but he is clearly no master of language, even at its simplest metaphorical level, for he continually says much more than he means. In the space of one short scene he has unwittingly made himself his competitor's confidant and financial aid. To add insult to injury, Horace remains ignorant of his interlocutor's identity only because of the false aristocratic family name to which Arnolphe holds so dearly, an incongruously hybrid sign not unlike those in which Tartuffe deals and seeks to reproduce (see below, Chapter 3). The label by which he had intended to elevate his dignity and social status has only deepened his involvement in an imbroglio that already threatens to entangle him in a kind of discourse for which he has no talent, the language of love. Not only is he in danger of being cuckolded; worse yet, he has to suffer Horace's discourse, for in order to avoid the fate he most fears, he has to augment his conspicuously slim body of knowledge. He must learn from Horace, submitting to him in dialogue in the very way he had refused vis-à-vis his friend Chrysalde. The pill of which he speaks is made all the more bitter by the portrait of a ridiculously jealous and crazy Monsieur de la Souche, with which Horace prefaces his story:

> Riche, à ce qu'on m'a dit, mais des plus sensés, non;
> Et l'on m'en a parlé comme d'un ridicule.
>
> . . .
>
> C'est un fou, n'est-ce pas?
> . . . Jaloux à faire rire? [I. iv. 330 ff.]

His torment is prolonged by a series of false exits, but in the end Arnolphe seems to reconcile himself to the humiliation of his new situation by reconsidering his position on other peoples' speech; he concludes that Horace talks too much and that he will profit from the chatter to once again become master of the situation:

> . . . pousser jusqu'au bout son caquet indiscret,
> Et savoir pleinement leur commerce secret. [I. iv. 365–66]

He has not at all changed his mind about owning and controlling Agnès, but has simply flipped the Port-Royal coin over, seeking through "discretion" — that is, well-timed silence, or that to which Agnès has recourse all through Act IV while she *acts* — to acquire enough knowledge to win out over Horace. In fact, he is prepared at the conclusion cf Act I to seek out his rival in order to learn more from him. It would seem that Arnolphe talks with those over whom he senses some dominion and listens to those who threaten his power.

At the beginning of Act II we find him for the first time in that same state in which he concludes the play:

> Ouf! Je ne puis parler, tant je suis prévenu:
> Je suffoque, et voudrais me pouvoir mettre nu. [II. ii. 393–44]

He claims to be so furious with his servants Alain and Georgette that he is linguistically incapacitated and momentarily mad. The difference between this scene and the final one, however, is that here he continues to speak, for in reality, he is hardly reduced to an inarticulate, "natural" or animal state, nor is he excluded from his self-created and self-defeating war for cultural domination. (Since he proposes to monopolize culture — generally defined as a network of systems of exchange — by using monologue he can neither win nor lose that war, for he has eliminated the possibility of an authentic other who might receive his triumphant meaning and thus validate it directly or indirectly.) He is just angry, not defeated; it would require some sort of final downfall vis-à-vis Horace and Agnès for him to succumb to that level of existence at which he would have liked to imprison his pupil. In scene v of Act II he finds himself obliged to liberate her from that prison of stupidity and inarticulateness. He has learned nothing from the servants (although the audience has learned that "La femme est en effet le potage de l'homme") and fears an unwitting show of emotion with Horace; so, ironically, he must learn the reality of the situation from Agnès. In order to do so, he will have to draw her out, to develop her discourse, for in reply to his questions, she only ticks off the entirely noncreative trifles to which he has rigidly limited her education:

> *Arnolphe:* La promenade est belle.
> *Agnès:* Fort belle.
> *Arnolphe:* Le beau jour!
> *Agnès:* Fort beau.
> *Arnolphe:* Quelle nouvelle?
> *Agnès:* Le petit chat est mort.
>
> . . .
>
> *Arnolphe:* Qu'avez-vous fait encor ces neuf ou dix jours-ci?
> *Agnès:* Six chemises, je pense, et six coiffes aussi. [II. v. 466 ff.]

Invoking the trusted "people-out-there-are-saying" tactic that Chrysalde tried in Act I, Arnolphe succeeds in unlocking the story which Agnès willingly unfolds at his bidding (lines 484 ff., Magné's "discours naïf").

Appropriately, her initial encounter with Horace is as much an apprenticeship in language as a first exposure to galantry. Her semiological naïveté manifests itself as total ignorance of metaphor, in the most general sense of that word. Although there is no precise indication in the text to that effect, it may well be that her long monologue beginning with line 484 constitutes her very first narration of any kind to anyone, and surely to Arnolphe.

If so, she has in Arnolphe's absence witnessed and participated in what is for her a remarkable demonstration of the exchange of signs, and apparently finds little difficulty in appropriating some of that demonstration for her own speech in his presence. While Arnolphe's literal and figural cloistering of Agnès protected her from the disease he most fears, it also destroyed her immunity, for she has proven herself particularly vulnerable, first to Horace's gestures, then to his words. She apparently did not immediately understand that his repeated greetings signify less a desire to be "civil," as she says, than to engage her in a kind of play which in its turn will signify to Horace that, yes, she is interested. The representativeness of a sign is comprehensible to her only on a literal or full level, that is, within the meaning the nuns or Arnolphe have assigned to it. She has learned that a bow or curtsy decodes to politeness, which in turn indicates good breeding, and therefore understands that signs can point to other signs as well as to things or concepts. However, she treats all his signs as indices, as a kind of phenomenal event to which she grants positive existence in the framework of a neatly defined social and semiological code, unaware for the moment that it solicits an understanding. In modern critical terms, she has cut out a whole area of immanence in the relationship between signs, their specifically figural potential. Horace has added something to his gesture, so that it has become intelligible only as metaphor within the new context of playful flirtation in which he has placed it. Language is not an objective phenomenon to which one can assign a standard truth-value, as Agnès seems to believe, but an exchange of signs open to interpretation, soliciting an understanding in a given context on the part of the "reader" or receiver. What is explicit in Horace's greeting is *there*, and therefore "true," but all that is implicit in his manner, and especially in the act of repetition, is equally present and therefore "true" in their exchange.

To use Paul de Man's terms, there is a kind of rhetorical blindness in Agnès's reading of Horace's signs,[28] for she intuitively grasps the nature of her exchange with Horace insofar as she is clearly in touch with her own strong attraction to him, but does not for the moment translate that understanding into words for Arnolphe. Her apprenticeship in semiology is still very new. She has totally missed the significance of Horace's reiterating his greeting, for between the first and the last bows, an evolution has already occurred in Horace's and Agnès's incipient relationship.

The comedy of repetition, like all repetition, is a temporal process assuming both resemblance and difference, for while the comedy lies in its function as a rigorous regulative principle, it denies any possibility of rigorous identity. If Horace's second greeting were exactly the same greeting as his first, he obviously could not repeat it several minutes later. If there is a difference between the two, as indeed there must be, it would not be illogical for someone as observant of Horace's beauty as Agnès appears to have been even at the outset, to wonder about the nature of the series of events in which she is involved. Horace is flirting with her, and while flirting back, she believes she is fulfilling a social obligation (or so she relates the incident to Arnolphe!).

The second part of Agnès's story (lines 503 ff.), her encounter with Horace's appointed go-between, follows the lesson in gesture with one in the figures of verbal language. The crux of the matter is of course the word "wound" (*blesser*). A mere convention in the galant's vocabulary, it would signify for anyone but Agnès "wounded with love" (*blessé d'amour*), pierced by Cupid's arrow, and so on. Once again Agnès hears a full, single-meaninged, decodable index, a sign whose objective truth lies in the rigidity of a clearly defined signified, the fact of having a wound on one's body, a signified which cannot vary with the context. She mistakes "signs of signs" for "signs of things," a confusing ambiguity indeed, according to Part II, chapter 14, of the Port-Royal *Logic*. In seventeenth-century terms, her readings are indeed "animal-like."

Throughout the *Meditations* and in his correspondence, Descartes "maintains that [human] language is available for the free expression of thought or for appropriate response in any new context,"[29] and the same principle underlies the Port-Royal *Grammar* and the *Logic*, these properties differentiating human signs from stimulus-prompted, context-bound animal responses.[30] Thus Agnès asks Horace's representative, "Did I drop something on his head?", to which the old woman, eager to serve her employer, only adds another series of metaphors:

> . . . vos yeux ont fait ce coup fatal,
> Et c'est de leurs regards qu'est venu tout son mal.
> [II. v. 517–18]

The figural value of the words "eyes," "fatal blow," "glances," and "pain" is lost on Agnès, and the old woman's task is rendered so much the easier, for she can now feel confident of the effect on Agnès of her talk of venom, of Horace's pining away, of cruel indifference and impending death. Agnès accepts as tragic this comic version of *Tristan and Isolde*, succumbing with an anguished: "What must I do to save him?" If her eyes did him harm and can save him, then she will see him as often as he wishes.

These are, once again, the "eyes" of a poetic convention totally foreign to Agnès, but Arnolphe immediately recognizes both the tragic imagery and the bringer of the philter ("Ah! sorcière maudite, empoisonneuse d'âmes, / Puisse l'enfer payer tes charitables trames!"), both the form and the content of the story. And he hardly wishes to play a comic King Mark. His quite literal psychic pain stems from his new-found knowledge of the situation, his consciousness of Agnès's now dangerous naïveté vis-à-vis metaphor and his uncertainty as to whether or not his will and passion are great enough to subdue the forces at work, that is, those of language, other peoples' continuing exchanges of signs. He decides, rightly or wrongly, that she is innocent of any bad faith, that she believes in her "cure" of Horace, and returns once again to his obsession: Has he or has he not been cuckolded? In his eagerness for a literal answer, he for a moment changes roles with Agnès (as the paths in their evolution have crossed at any rate) and entirely misses the importance of her pleasure at Horace's verbal caresses. Inattentive to her experience of the sensuous joy of sound and metaphor, he is intent upon looking for a single signified:

> . . . des mots les plus gentils du monde,
> Des choses que jamais rien ne peut égaler,
> Et dont, toutes les fois que je l'entends parler,
> La douceur me chatouille et là dedans remue
> Certain je ne sais quoi dont je suis toute émue.
>
> . . .
>
> Outre tous ces discours, toutes ces gentillesses,
> Ne vous faisait-il point aussi quelques caresses? [II. v. 560 ff.]

The ribbon Agnès has given Horace, as important a sign of her submission as her unexplained trembling at Horace's verbal touch, is a mere trifle to Arnolphe compared to what he feared lost. Concerned with the new level of existence which Agnès has attained, but not cognizant of the irrevocable nature of her experience, he attempts to reassert their relationship by claiming her physical person in marriage. He does not understand that his will and his words can no longer dominate her, for her very identity has undergone modification in his absence and in her apprenticeship to metaphor and dialogue. The desire she heard in Horace's voice and words, although she does not understand precisely *what* he desires, and the pleasure they provoked in her have afforded her the beginning of an awareness of entire semiotic systems: figures and tropes, sexuality, personality, and, not least of all, her discursive potential, a system of identities and differences which Arnolphe cannot destroy. His only hope must be a return to physical cloistering, for her linguistic and sexual sophistication can henceforth only blossom. And her skill in finding ways to contact Horace will increase proportionately. Arnolphe's orders to turn him away and his refusal to suffer any further discussion with her at the end of the scene are effective only for a brief moment. The line from Corneille's *Sertorius* that closes the scene might refer directly to my third epigraph, for it signifies both itself as instrument ("Je suis maître [car] je parle") as well as the absolute power that always constitutes the goal of Arnolphe's monologues ("allez, obéissez").

All the successive vicissitudes of everyone's fortune in Act III reflect Arnolphe's refusal to see that he is no longer master, that in fact the struggle has been relocated to a new battlefield, symbolized by the letter-enveloped stone Agnès has thrown to Horace between Acts II and III. Arnolphe's opening speech of Act III, a strikingly verbose sigh of relief because Horace has been barred from the house, is all the more ironic in view of the young man's mockery in scene iv of such strong-arm tactics. This battle will not be won with stone fortresses or swords, and Horace understands the uselessness of such feudal weaponry in the age of the logos:

> Cet homme gendarmé d'abord contre mon feu,
> Qui chez lui se retranche et de grès fait parade,
> Comme si j'y voulais entrer par escalade. [III. iv. 927–79]

Stone walls and brute force can imprison Agnès's person but have hardly blocked the flow of signs between her and Horace. However, since it is with physical possession that he is wholly and exclusively concerned, he sees in the letter more a danger of losing Agnès bodily than a warning about the manner in which she is being seduced. If the fact that the stone which Arnolphe would have protect his power and possessions becomes a vehicle for communication between the young lovers inspires hearty laughter in Horace, it does not alter Arnolphe's disposition in the least. Even thematically, the plot has moved to a level of figure and metaphor, a level at which people are persuaded with rhetoric, where will conquers in verbs, not in armor. Arnolphe appears a parody of the knightly man of action, for he lacks the doctrine, the "courtoisie," without which his tactics and accoutrements are simply barbarously funny, to the point of incongruence and meaninglessness. He in fact becomes the "animal" of the play, as Horace points out in line 958; he cannot accede to the cultural and, specifically, linguistic level on which all of the other characters, except Alain and Georgette, exist. It is in this sense that he is an obstacle, for he would prevent Agnès from learning first how to speak, then how to write, and, those measures failing, he would interrupt any flow of language between her and Horace. To that extent, he of course understands the danger of figure and metaphor, but fails to use them himself with sufficient address to modify his relations with Agnès or to affect his rivalry with Horace.

Rather than learn to use rhetoric, which implies learning the art of thinking, Arnolphe will go so far as to impose silence on Agnès in his presence (Act II, scene v, and virtually all of Act III) and to imprison her in his absence. He cuts off her speech, which he calls "noise" (lines 639–41), at the end of Act II and becomes increasingly noisy himself in the course of Act III, his monologues growing in length, if not in depth, as his hold on Agnès decreases. Expositor (lines 675–746) and would-be exegete ("Je vous expliquerai ce que cela veut dier" [line 751]; "Je vous expliquerai ces choses comme il faut" [line 803]), he will tolerate the sound of Agnès's voice only to hear her read a text of which the anonymous author might have been himself, that is, to forcibly alienate her discourse.

Of the ten "Maximes du mariage" read, only the first, which treats of the husband's ownership, is stated positively. The remaining nine are proscriptive: vanity (except for one's husband's benefit), callers, presents, writing tables, paper and ink, *salons*, gaming, and pastoral outings are all forbidden. The tautological nature of the maxims is obvious, even striking; they all mean exactly what the first one prescribes, but would reinforce it negatively. Arnolphe is clearly more concerned with cuckoldry than with sexual fidelity. These are not the Ten Commandments, but nine ways to disobey the first. We know, in fact, from his first conversation with Horace, that Arnolphe long fancied himself a gifted undoer of husbandly peace of mind, and his experience is reflected in maxims two through ten. His lack of psychological insight vis-à-vis Agnès is equally a linguistic oversight. According to the *Grammar*: "Il n'y a point d'objet dans le monde hors de notre esprit, qui réponde à la particule *non*; mais il est clair qu'elle ne marque autre chose que le jugement que nous faisons, qu'une chose n'est pas une autre."[31] The words used to negate do not correspond, like affirmative judgments, to mental concepts reflecting objective reality or to desires reflecting the "mouvements de notre âme,"[32] but are rather freakishly pure signs, in that they represent nothing. They are simply mental erasers, capable of undoing affirmation, "la principale manière de notre pensée."[33] For the "messieurs" of Port-Royal, then, affirmation is pre-sumed in negation, grammatically precedes it, and remains implicit in it:

> Arnauld et Lancelot semblent en éffet considérer la négation non pas logiquement comme ce qui sépare le sujet de son attribut, mais grammaticalement comme un des accidents du verbe (comparable aux notions de personne, de nombre, etc.) qui, exprimé par un mot séparé n'altèrerait qu'accessoirement (et au regard de l'ensemble de la proposition) le sens et la fonction de la liaison verbale; celle-ci resterait alors affirmative.[34]

In seventeenth-century linguistic terms, Arnolphe has presented Agnès with nine concepts, to which he indeed adds a negative imperative, but which, because that addition has no ontological value, remain at the outset propositions containing new ideas for Agnès. The grammatical and ontological bond that joins negation to affirmation lends considerable ambiguity to Arnolphe's sermon. He has in fact given her one rule and nine means of transgressing it. In his terror of hermeneutics, of interpretation as metaphor, or of *any* new text, he instructs her not to draw any conclusions about what the maxims mean, in fact forbidding her to understand them, for he will explain them to her himself.

One wonders about this separation of reading and interpretation, of language and metaphor; it is the words on the page, which he instructs her to read one by one ("Vous achéverez seule, et pas à pas . . ." [line 802]), that solicit a "reading" or understanding. Their very imminence and the act of reading itself imply interpretation or, rather, are synonymous with it, as in English when we say: "Do you read me?" for "Do you understand?", or in French, "M'entendez-vous?" for "Me comprenez-vous?" The perception of a sign is necessarily my interpretation of it. Agnès cannot finish her "word for word" reading without seeing, hearing, and grasping nine ways to re-establish a contact she enjoys and misses.

Arnolphe's longest speech, the "piece of wax" monologue (III. iii), situated at the exact center of the play, thus provides both another moment of delightful irony turned on Arnolphe — Agnès is indeed malleable, if only Arnolphe understood the nature of language and the way in which it impresses or imprints itself — and a pivotal point in the dual struggle with Agnés and Horace. Coming from a moment of considerable blindness, and moving toward an equally comic lack of insight and downright disaster with Horace, he heartily congratulates himself. His victory was in fact a very long monologue containing one proposition: "I will own you" or, flipped over, "Thou shalt not commit cuckoldry." Since he has succeeded in preventing her from responding in any way, he assumes that she is a soft chip of wax in his hands, that he can turn her will in any direction he wishes. Just as he does not understand the implications of the premise that language is necessarily the expression of thought, so he cannot see that thought and feeling cannot exist without language as a potential for its enunciation. What Agnès was probably thinking in Act III, scene ii, she may very well write to Horace, as indeed she has already enunciated other thoughts and feelings to him.

The letter that Horace reads to Arnolphe in Act III, scene iv, would indicate that it is not the act of writing that is dangerous to Arnolphe, but rather Agnès's new-found awareness of her own feelings. In an age when epistemology begins as the object of an intuition, and when writing is purely phonetic, a transcription of the acoustic symbols used in speech, Agnès's letter appears a necessary and logical result of her first encounter with Horace. In the evolution from the *Discourse on Method* to the *Meditations*, it becomes apparent that one of the constants facilitating access to Descartes' thought is the absolute inseparability of the notions of intuition, deduction, and order. Method consists of discovering the simple, the fundamental ontological unit, which is the object of an intuition, situating it in an order (according to rational order), and then progressing by degrees in this rational, orderly manner to knowledge of the complex. Without intuition, order would not exist, because it would have no substance. Without order, intuitions would present themselves in a purely random fashion, as fragmentary experiences, and, even as a group, could hardly constitute knowledge. What Agnès "knows" during and after she meets Horace, she knows intuitively, that is, by virtue of her God-given capacity to think and feel. She does not have a method and is hardly in search of science, but the chain-of-events style in which Cartesian epistemology describes what we experience as one event and call by any one of the links' names in the chain, nevertheless also describes Agnès's linguistic acculturation. She automatically feels, deduces, and organizes into rational discourse simply because she is human, that is, was created by God in his image. Whoever taught her to write down that discourse, such ability remains insignificant per se.

The preamble to the *Grammar* makes it clear that writing's only function is to give duration to words which the air might otherwise dissipate, for grammar is defined as speaking:

> La Grammaire est l'Art de parler.
> Parler est expliquer ses pensées par
> des signes, que les hommes ont
> inventés à ce dessein.
> On a trouvé que les plus commodes de ces
> signes étaient les sons et la voix.
> Mais parce que ces sons passent, on a
> inventé d'autres signes pour les
> rendre durables et visibles, qui sont
> les caractères de l'écriture . . .[35]

What is significant, as Agnès herself says, is that she has some thoughts and would like Horace to know them ("J'ai des pensées que je désirerais que vous sussiez"). The ability to express her thoughts, however naïvely, is as automatic as are the thoughts themselves. Although she is as yet incapable of effectively invoking figure and metaphor, she has deduced from her interviews with Horace that she has heretofore been held in total ignorance of people and of human commerce, or has rather immediately sensed that lack in experiencing pleasure at his metaphorical and literal caresses. With him she learned that she lives in a universe of figure and metaphor, and that she had simply been prevented from participating. Her letter avows an ignorance of the means of participation, but expresses a strong desire to do so. She would like to learn the art of speaking (writing) and to know if Horace is sincere.

34

Given Agnès's humanity, her initial exposure to an attractive young man, and the power of pens over swords, Arnolphe's enterprise is clearly doomed in Act III. It is his inability to recognize defeat, and his accompanying refusal to give up, that keep the plot and the homology "speech-knowledge-domination" rebounding for two more acts, reinforcing the comedy of the same. Arnolphe will continue, as he says, to try to

> mettre un ordre et dedans et dehors
> Qui du godelureau rompe tous les efforts. [IV. i. 1010–11]

Since, in Cartesian terms, order is a function of intuition before it manifests itself as the product of action in the world, and inside and outside are qualities of language rather than of fortresses, he can neither hope to succeed nor surrender to his rival. For this reason, and because Horace is as inept at using force as Arnolphe is ignorant of the verbal universe in which he lives, the play must end in a stalemate, and a rather Cartesian one at that; while Arnolphe possesses Agnès's person in the final scene, her thoughts, desires, and language, all faculties of the "âme," are directed toward Horace. Only Enrique's and Oronte's arrival and the revelation of Agnès's identity — of the semiotic group or class system in which she should rightfully be allowed participation — (if she is Oronte's daughter, how can she henceforth be forced to live as an animal or slave?) — prove capable of converting the existing stalemate into an authentic checkmate of Arnolphe's monopolistic enterprise.

# A Certain Theory
## of Representation

> . . . puisqu'on doit discourir des choses et non pas des mots, et que la plupart des contrariétés viennent de ne pas entendre et d'envelopper dans un même mot des choses opposées, il ne faut qu'ôter le voile de l'équivoque, et regarder ce qu'est la comédie en soi, pour voir si elle est condamnable.
>
> — Preface to *Tartuffe*, 1669

> Au XVII⁰ et au XVIII⁰ siècle, l'existence propre du langage, sa vieille solidité de chose inscrite dans le monde étaient dissoutes dans le fonctionnement de la représentation; tout langage valait comme discours.
>
> — Michel Foucault,
> *Les Mots et les choses*[1]

Much has been made of the play on and interplay between "appearances" and "reality" in *Tartuffe*. Hypocrisy is a mask whose capacity for blocking real or sincere communication with the other characters in the play threatens the happiness of those characters and the very order of their universe. It matters little that Tartuffe's mask is transparent to everyone but Mme Pernelle and Orgon; the latter's absolute power as head-of-household and his unconditional surrender of personal, religious, familial, and financial responsibility to his idol and surrogate create an untenable situation for everyone except Orgon and Tartuffe. Damis is in danger not only of losing both his inheritance and Valère's sister but of exile from the family; Mariane may be forced to renounce her beloved to marry someone she abhors; and Elmire, abandoned by her spouse, finds herself avidly pursued by Tartuffe. The crisis can only be resolved by a revelation of the truth. The mask must be ripped off, as Damis would have it, reasoned away in Cléante's manner, or the hypocrite seduced into allowing it to fall, a feat Elmire successfully accomplishes on two occasions, first unwittingly and then purposefully (III. iii, and IV. v). The assumption on which the entire play rests is that truth does indeed exist and is therefore available, that the seeker has only to eliminate the obstacles blocking his path to it or tear away the veil that conceals it.

Comedy, argues Molière in his 1669 preface, is in *reality* a "poème ingénieux qui, par des leçons agréables, reprend les défauts des hommes."[2] Such is its thingness, true nature, or real status. It is by deforming the definition, by wrapping up different and contradictory meanings in a single word, that his enemies have succeeded in dropping an equivocal veil over comedy's essential clarity, and thus in stigmatizing the genre in general and prohibiting *Tartuffe* in particular. Similarly, evil men corrupt the most saintly of things: philosophy is abused into supporting impious doctrines; piety is exploited in the most criminal interests. A righteous man can avoid the pitfalls of fallacy, lie, and disguise, however, by making certain clear distinctions: "On n'enveloppe point dans une fausse conséquence la bonté des choses que l'on corrompt, avec la malice des corrupteurs. On sépare toujours le mauvais usage d'avec l'intention de l'art."[3] Comedy's mask — costuming, set design, fictitious characters speaking contrived lines — remains morally justifiable because its goal is praiseworthy: it veils reality only for a moment, with the single purpose of serving the truth through an art form.

Tartuffe's costume, gestures, and speech are, quite to the contrary, intended to serve the very hypocrisy of which they are both the signifier and signified. The real persona behind his mask is criminal, as the audience easily discerns by the very grotesqueness of his performance. As J. D. Hubert points out, Tartuffe is a rather poor actor, and only Orgon's craving for a spectacle created and produced by himself assures the impostor an audience.[4] His performance informs the audience and everyone in Orgon's household of his true nature, and because of this awareness, his nature similarly indicates his mask. Orgon, like the enemies of whom Molière speaks in his preface, sees only the signifier or performance, while everyone else perceives signifier and signified as a whole, as a representation of fraud. Molière thus argues that comedy constitutes a unique kind of sign in that it indicates a truth which may be and often is very different from the disguise it employs, and that Tartuffe, in using fraudulent behavior to perpetrate fraud, is not only immoral but a threat to the art form. His suggested remedy is a clear distinction between good and evil uses of the same signifier, a distinction which would in turn remove all blocks to the signified, *giving access to the true nature of things.*

Indeed, the notion of representation, true or false, finds itself thematically at the center of the play. Emphasized in the plot by a crisis situation and the urgent need for an exaggeratedly clear demonstration of the difference between truth and sham, it reappears both implicitly and explicitly in everyone's linguistic and gestural behavior. "L'être" must triumph over the "paraître," as Jacques Guicharnaud points out,[5] and the comedy that reader and audience enjoy takes the form of each character's reaction to that absolute necessity. It is not only Orgon's faulty perception of things and his correlative need to see and touch their "reality" in order to believe in their existence that are in question, but also his judgment. The text's relationship to the Port-Royal *Logic* is thus inverse. Presenting itself as a guide to the art of thinking correctly — that is, logically — the latter treats principally of judgment and its expressive form, the proposition. However, the status of judgment is essentially ambiguous in the *Logic.* As I noted in Chapter 1, the *Logic* inherits and accepts the Port-Royal *Grammar* theory of the verb, the assumption that men never speak simply to state their perceptions of things, but to affirm and judge them. This essential bond between propositions and things necessitates careful prior consideration of ideas or of the perceptions on which verbs act. The copula is also an act, the principle act of which language is capable:

> . . . c'est la liaison-action qui en constitue la condition nécessaire (du jugement) et on ne parlera de jugement qu'au moment où le verbe introduira, dans une série de termes, l'acte de liaison et d'affirmation: en ce sens, il y a une distinction radicale entre juger et concevoir, entre parler et nommer. Mais en même temps, tout jugement "enfermera" des conceptions. Le jugement ne s'effectuera que si le verbe relie des termes-objets: il n'est pas possible de juger sans concevoir.[6]

Just as the *Logic* must consider the nature of ideas and perceptions in order to discuss judgment, so we cannot speak of Orgon's faulty perceptions in seventeenth-century linguistic terms without considering the nature of his judgments.

In so doing we find them surprisingly similar. Orgon saw Tartuffe praying, therefore the proposition, "Tartuffe is a pious man." There is little transition from idea to proposition, from the particular to the general, from perception to reality. Orgon not only believes what he sees; he simultaneously makes of that perception an attribute, an act on a subject, creating Tartuffe from a gesture executed at the moment he first saw him. The generalization then blossoms into another judgment on the reality of things and the world: "Tartuffe est demeuré le 'tout' d'Orgon. Voir Tartuffe est pour Orgon voir l'univers. . . . Ce sont les gestes sensibles de Tartuffe qui experiment la vérité du monde."[7] Similarly, he will seek to destroy the impostor upon perceiving his attempt at cuckoldry. Elmire's agonized but ineffectual coughing and Tartuffe's subsequent offer of some licorice juice mark Orgon's uncertainty vis-à-vis his own perception (and a correspondingly literal acceptance of the role assigned to him by his wife), not a hesitation to judge hypocrisy. For the first time in the play he experiences some difficulty in believing what his senses record, increasing the comedy inherent in the situation; but, once convinced, his judgment proves as immediate and irrevocable as his first was. Tartuffe is henceforth as evil as he was pious before the scene in question.

The analogy between things as they are in the world and reality as it exists in an individual character's "true nature" is hardly a gratuitous one. Not only in his argument for comedy and for the play *Tartuffe,* but also in the text of that play, Molière presents both logical definition, whose function it is to describe the correct signified, and human nature as available but inaccessible. Comedy and Tartuffe exist and can therefore be known; the opaque screen behind which they are hidden, however, renders them temporarily absent for us, in the case of comedy, and for Orgon and Mme Pernelle in Tartuffe's case. It is clear insofar as *Tartuffe* is concerned that Molière sees mistakes about the signified as traceable to misrepresentation. Deliberate, malicious fraud on someone's part conceals half of the sign and substitutes a foreign element for it, thereby dislocating the sign's ontological value and crippling the interpreter's capacity to place a logically correct judgment on it. The copula and attribute cannot act happily upon an idea which has been falsified or remains itself unclear. The Port-Royal *Logic* opens with just such an emphasis:

> Comme nous ne pouvons avoir aucune connais-
> sance de ce qui est hors de nous que par l'entremise des
> idées qui sont en nous, les réflexions que l'on peut faire
> sur nos idées sont peut-être ce qu'il y a de plus important
> dans la Logique, parce que c'est le fondement de tout le
> reste.[8]

However, clarity of ideas can only be reached through an understanding of their nature. There are indeed ideas of things and
ideas of signs,[9] definitions of things and definitions of words,[10]
and it is essential to distinguish these two facets of representation — the one simple, "comme l'idée de la terre, du soleil," the
other complex, as when "on ne regarde un certain objet que
comme en représentant un autre . . ."[11] It is thus that meaning
in classical French epistemology becomes a strictly binary play
described by the boundaries of the sign. Even as it indicates a
signified, the signifier reflects back on itself, assuming responsibility for the sign as a whole, and the signified begins to resemble
a referent: ". . . le signe enferme deux idées: l'une de la chose qui
représente; l'autre de la chose représentée; et sa nature consiste
à exciter la seconde par la première."[12]

If falsifying a sign necessitates the violation of its complex
integrity as indicator and indicated, as both part and whole, so
does any reading of it. The study and analysis of representation
contained in the *Grammar* and *Logic* poses less the problem of
the sign's relationship to the referent than that of its internal
structure and coherence, of how it is linked to its own signified.
The commentary on judgment centers around a theory of verbs
which treats essentially of the copula, of the liaison between subject and attribute, just as chapter 4, Part I, of the *Logic*, "Des
Idées des choses et des idées des signes," discusses and orders
signs according to their manner of binding together signifier and
signified. Signs differ in relation to their signified according to
the origin of the tie (natural or conventional), the kind of tie
(the sign may or may not be part of the whole it designates), and
its relative certitude (respiration is always a sign of life, but a pale
complexion may or may not indicate pregnancy).[13] These three
criteria in turn determine a sign's utility for empirical knowledge;
that is its role in the relationship between things and words. At
the same time, things and words must go their separate ways in
such a strictly binary or representational view of language. Language does not leave an indelible mark on the world, but says

what is to the best of its ability, and, correlatively, is no more than it says. Its function is to name things and to name names. The earth is called "earth" and then encased in other secondary names, descriptive or decorative, such as "round," "solid," "dwelling," etc. It is the representativeness of the sign that is in question in this fundamental duplicity:

> . . . en son essence propre, la représentation est toujours perpendiculaire à elle-même: elle est à la fois *indication* et *apparaître*; rapport à un objet et manifestation de soi. A partir de l'âge classique, le signe c'est la représentativité de la représentation en tant qu'elle est *représentable*.[14]

Significantly, the *Logic* gives the map or chart as its example of a pure sign — one whose signified is its own representational value. Its only content is what it represents — that is, a spatial distribution — and the representation of that space can itself only be represented by lines and words, or, again, representation. Thus the exemplary sign both indicates and manifests itself, is both double and doubles back on itself, such that, while alone it could represent nothing, once the signifier is linked to a signified, it describes the representativeness and meaning of the sign.

Such a theory of signs clearly locates meaning not in the relationship between words as appearances and reality as truth but within language itself, in a discourse which is its own appearance and reality. The dislocation of the sign of which Molière speaks in his Preface constitutes a displacement within the realm of discourse, a twisting of logic, rather than, strictly speaking, a misrepresentation of reality. In stating that signs may be either "certain" or "probable," either inherent in and part of what they designate or linked to it in a purely arbitrary manner,[15] classical doctrine defines language as both the result of analytical thought and its instrument. For a sign to be a sign it must both include itself in its signifier in such a way as to become an integral part of it and, at the same time, remain separate and distinct from it. A sign cannot function if it does not present itself to our minds simultaneously with the idea it represents; by the same token, however, its power to designate is directly proportional to the clarity with which it can extricate itself from that idea in order to indicate it. Respiration is a sign of life. It constitutes one element of an animal's vital functions, but cannot designate that vitality unless isolated from it, from the whole in which it functions as thing. The relationship between signs and things is thus fundamentally equivocal: some signs, such as breathing and life, are identifiable as integrated empirical phenomena; others, such as pallor and pregnancy, are entirely separate empirical events; but all must be extracted and remain isolated from that empirical reality or their own "thingness" in order for representativeness, or discourse, to exist.

It is by virtue of an analysis of the world that signs are constituted and appear to us as such; once endowed with representative power, they in turn assure the continuation of the analytical process, eternally surrounding signs with more signs, isolating and encircling, combining and dispersing. Signs, whether empirically identifiable or purely arbitrary analogues for that which they represent (such as the word "triangle" for a three-sided geometric figure), afford an identity to things, enabling them to become distinct and then to establish relationships between and among them. In this sense, equivocation is a *sine qua non* of representativeness. Comedy cannot be isolated and defined without first belonging to some confused whole, without the existence of multiple definitions against which Molière places his own selected one. It is in the interplay between things and signs, *as that interplay is described and describable in discourse*, that human judgment originates.

The portraits in *Tartuffe* are a striking example of the ambiguity described above, which is both fundamental to and implicit in the representation of deliberate misrepresentation in a world of discourse whose very essence and *sine qua non* are precisely representation. In the course of Act I, Dorine, Damis, Mariane, Elmire, and Cléante are caricatured by Mme Pernelle, after which the same lady paints Tartuffe, who is absent. Damis and Dorine counter with their own portraits of Tartuffe, to which Dorine adds a portrait of the neighbors Daphné and Orante. In scene ii, once Mme Pernelle has left, Cléante dares offer one of her, and Dorine generously elaborates hers of Tartuffe, describing Orgon in the process. The entire series is capped, in scene v, by Orgon's famous portrait of Tartuffe: "C'est un homme...qui ...ha! un homme...un homme enfin" (I. v. 272). All of these portraits are double-edged swords in that they reveal both some aspect or selected aspects of the person described and the portraitist himself. Through them we discover respectively Mme

Pernelle's rather narrow allegiance to her son and to the doctrine and the man he has espoused; Damis's reckless and Dorine's more prudent refusal to submit; Mariane's timidity; and, finally, Elmire's and Cléante's separate brands of "honnêteté." At the same time, the elements composing the portraits, although often exaggerated and distorted because of choices of words or the nature of the portrait itself, are not entirely inapplicable. The play demonstrates that Dorine is in fact "une fille suivante un peu trop forte en gueule" (13–14) by contemporary standards, that Damis can be a "méchant garnement" (19), that Mariane, "la discrète," does lead a social life which Mme Pernelle finds reprehensible, that Elmire is "dépensière" (29), and that Cléante is a "prêcheur de maximes" (37). If we consider the portraits as classically economical efforts to define experienced reality,[16] the descriptive elements contained in them fall into the Port-Royal category of ideas or definitions of things and not into that of ideas of signs. However, since the "reality" described is a person, the question of self and other, of essence or personality and of how one character experiences another, immediately arises.

On what are the portraitists juxtaposing names? Elmire's portrait of Damis would certainly differ from Mme Pernelle's, and we can scarcely imagine a truly exhaustive one of him. The center of the tiny circle of signs which is the portrait remains difficult to locate, for, at the very least, it varies considerably according to the speaker. In this sense, the characters themselves, in relation to each other, function like "signs" whose "meaning" is unclear. The speaker, in turn, may indicate, reveal, or designate something or things about himself through his portrait (Mme Pernelle's eagerness to make harsh moral judgments, Dorine's boldness and humor), but does not signify himself in any whole sense. Certain of the portraits prove true as far as they go when related to a character's subsequent behavior, but only if we see that behavior as illustrative a posteriori of a sign or catalogue of signs. It is in the interrelationship between the verbal and physical signs a character displays and the group of signs another character has used to describe him that the truth or error, the representative value, of a portrait is established.

While the question of the representativeness and representability of signs remains hypothetical for those characters whose portraits are not discussed, it is clearly posed in the case of Tartuffe, around whom the whole debate turns. In line 42 the former first describes him as "un homme de bien," to which Damis retorts with "un cagot de critique" (45). Dorine subsequently describes him as "ce critique zélé" (51), "un inconnu" (62), and "un gueux qui . . . n'avait pas de souliers / Et dont l'habit entier valait bien dix deniers" (63–64). In line 59 Damis interjects "ce pied plat" into the portrait, reinforcing Dorine's response to the "homme de bien" claim. When Mme Pernelle remains unshaken, Dorine decides to openly suggest Tartuffe's attraction to Elmire: "Je crois que de Madame il est, ma foi, jaloux" (84).

Each of these diametrically opposed attempts at portraying the impostor aims at an orderly, almost crystalline summation, in as few words as possible, of the case for or against Tartuffe. Since Mme Pernelle, like her son, will not be swayed by verbal evidence, Dorine and Damis are forced to draw out, then exceed, their portraits with fairly long descriptions and arguments (85–140). At that point, Cléante, whose forte is hardly concision, can intervene in an altogether apropos manner (93).

The vain efforts to close the debate as briefly and victoriously as possible are indicative in their superimposition of a clearly defined order upon the "reality" of Tartuffe. Mme Pernelle maintains that he is *really* and *essentially* an "homme de bien" whose intention it is to lead the family along the road to Heaven (53); the others reply that, on the contrary, he is really a fraud, a dangerous opportunist, and a lecher. Thus the relationship and possible similarity between Tartuffe and the portraits that would represent him comes into question in the heat of the debate. If, beginning in Act III, Tartuffe successfully illustrates Dorine's and Damis's representations of him, even surpassing them at times, at this point in the play we can only see that relationship from the opposite angle: To what extent are the verbal sketches signs and indications of his behavior and character? Here, in order to be certified as "true," a portrait must *resemble* Tartuffe, whoever he is (and that, for the moment, is the problem at hand).

The text speaks to us, however, from a period when resemblance is, as Michel Foucault points out, highly suspect as prima facie evidence of sameness, and is rather valorized and appreciated for its illusory quality: ". . . partout se dessinent les chimères de la similitude, mais on sait que ce sont des chimères; c'est le temps privilégié du trompe-l'œil, de l'illusion comique,

44

du théâtre, du quiproquo, des songes et visions."[17] In baroque terms, similarity constitutes both a dangerous trap, in the quest for certainty, and an entertaining game of the mind and senses when recognized as such. Scientific method concerns itself with the former, whereas art, and theater in particular, is concerned with the latter. However, in a theater which claims to be "un poème ingénieux, qui par des leçons agréables, reprend les défauts des hommes,"[18] the status of resemblance becomes equivocal, for it represents the search for certain knowledge in the comic register and as a baroque art form. The audience realizes long before they see him that Tartuffe is an impostor, that he will probably wear some sort of verbal mask and continually seek to create an illusion, a theatrical performance whose relation to real events in the real world is dubious. Orgon's family must nevertheless prove for certain that he is a hypocrite, and their first attempt to do so produces the portraits in Act I. It is by using plays on similarity as both recognized, pleasurable occasions for error and dangerous critical obstacles to truth that Molière, by equivocating their status, seeks to create an entertainment form that also functions as the defender of the Good and the Right, and thus to justify comedy's existence. In *Tartuffe* this equivocation takes the form of various attempts to establish and prove the impostor's real identity, to demonstrate the hazards of re-presentation, but in a representational mode. Molière presents Tartuffe as a scoundrel, first by Dorine's and Damis's descriptions and then by his own words and acts, but Tartuffe represents himself as a pious man.

It is entirely consistent that the ambiguous truth-illusion relationship and its link to the notion of similarity should show up in the very methods the characters use to counteract Mme Pernelle's stubbornness in Act I. Their aim seems to be to draw a portrait so true, so representative of Tartuffe, that she will begin to question her unconditional faith in him. The problem is, of course, that they see him differently and so must convince her with similarities of the dangers of similarity as a means of knowing. Such an art of persuasion brings to mind Descartes' *Regulae*, which open with the statement "Les hommes ont l'habitude, chaque fois qu'ils découvrent une ressemblance entre deux choses, de leur attribuer à l'une et à l'autre, même en ce qui les distingue, ce qu'ils ont reconnu vrai de l'une d'elles."[19] Significantly, this warning introduces a rule he entitles "Le But des études doit être de diriger l'esprit pour qu'il porte des jugements solides et vrais sur tout ce qui se présente à lui." Mme Pernelle has seen Tartuffe chastise the family for their unseemly behavior and heard him speak of self-flagellation. She has correlated these perceptions with a preconceived notion of piety, attributing the former both to the genuine "dévot" and to Tartuffe. Speaking in the same terms, Dorine tries to point out that Tartuffe does not resemble a pious man at all, for saints do not take over the control of family life, profit from their benefactors' affluence, and covet people's wives. However surprising it may seem to view a common sense maid as a spokesman for Cartesian methodology, it is Dorine who, in lines 69 and 70, first bases the effort to correct Mme Pernelle's faulty judgment on a clear and evident intuition, the only possible point of departure for logical deduction according to the *Regulae*. It may be noted that Descartes' Rule III begins: "Sur les objets proposés à notre étude il faut chercher, non ce que d'autres ont pensé ou ce que nous-mêmes nous conjecturons, mais ce dont nous pouvons avoir l'intuition claire et évidente ou ce que nous pouvons déduire avec certitude: car ce n'est pas autrement que la science s'acquiert."[20] For Dorine, and herein lie the comedy of her "science" and the incongruous quality of my comparison, the statement: "Tout son fait, croyez-moi, n'est rien qu'hypocrisie" (70), is as self-evident a truth as thought, existence, and the three-sidedness of triangles. She would like to start from that simple fact, interpreting Tartuffe's behavior and deducing his motives in the manner which must follow logically.

The stipulations of Rules V and VI might be resumed as follows:

1. Method consists in the ordering and disposing of things to discover some truth.

2. To conform to method we must gradually reduce complicated, obscure propositions to the most simple ones imaginable.

3. We must start from the intuition of these simple propositions and progress by degrees to the knowledge of all the others.

4. In each series of things in which we have deduced some truth, we must select the most simple thing and see how close to or far from it the others stand,

thus deciding how the more complex things are related to one another.[21]

Of all the confused and conflicting information so far at our disposal (Tartuffe's harsh criticism, his wish to guide the family into salvation, his poverty and peasantlike appearance, the existing family crisis and the division into camps, the neighbors' gossip), the most simple piece offered is Dorine's statement, "Tartuffe is a hypocrite." She would order and arrange all the rest in relation to that proposition, although in fact, and necessarily so in view of seventeenth-century class structures, the task of actually ordering things, of deducing a logical series, is relegated to Cléante in scene v. The order she and Damis impose in scene i is limited to the selected elements of which they compose their portrait-caricature, a kind of pseudo-scientifically certified resemblance, the paradoxical superposition of fact and representation.

Thus the portraits suggest a comic image of the entire classical *epistēmē*. In them we find a constant reshuffling of acts of comparison to make of them instruments for knowing, the identification of atomic elements from which to build logical series as well as the correlative absolute quality given to those fundamental intuitions, and, finally, an attempt to differentiate sameness and difference by establishing the latter: "En ce sens, le discernement impose à la comparaison la recherche première et fondamentale de la différence: se donner par l'intuition une représentation distincte des choses, et saisir clairement le passage nécessaire d'un élément de la série à celui qui lui succède immédiatement."[22] When in scene ii of Act I Dorine describes Orgon, Tartuffe, and the nature of their relationship, she immediately establishes a comparison between what she is about to say and Cléante's preceding, one-line portrait of Mme Pernelle: ". . . que de son Tartuffe elle paraît coiffée!" (I. ii. 178). Surprisingly enough, Cléante, who most often displays a marked propensity for speech-making, also offers the most concise, crystalline portrait in the play. Archetypal in its selection of a single image, it summarizes and represents Mme Pernelle in so powerful a manner that we are struck by the resemblance, precisely because the similarity between the image and the woman we have just seen is so seductive, regardless of its possibly illusory quality.

Dorine then proceeds to simultaneously establish the difference between and identity of mother and son via a dual com-

parison, first explicitly by suggesting the degree of their infatua-
tion with Tartuffe and Orgon's daily involvement with him (lines
179 and 185–99), and then implicitly in a long, well-embellished,
often repetitive description. Her aim here is not to strike a de-
cisive blow in a critical debate, but rather to fill in the audience.
She therefore surrounds her statement, "Tartuffe is a hypocrite,"
with more statements: implications, examples, explanations, and
simple decoration. As method prescribes, Dorine the comic
logician first establishes a difference between Orgon and Mme
Pernelle: "Oh! vraiment tout cela n'est rien au prix du fils . . ."
(I. ii. 179), and then goes on to a series of comparisons that
have nothing to do with the latter, for she is not a character
about whom we need information. It is therefore logical in
Dorine's terms — and for the plot — to go on to the son, so that
any comic image of methodical deduction disappears from her
description. Orgon of the Fronde is compared to Orgon today,
who is compared to an "homme hébété" (183). Thus Dorine
provides us with an explanation: Tartuffe's hypocrisy is dangerous because the head of the household has been totally trans-
formed by it and remains under the spell. In a sense, she suggests
a portrait in the lines:

> . . . il est devenu comme un homme hébété,
> Depuis que de Tartuffe on le voit entêté . . . [183–84]

She proceeds to use the rest of her speech to fill in detail,
with heavy emphasis on certain lines. There was a kind of logical
progression from her self-evident declaration of Tartuffe's hypocrisy to the picture of the effect he has had on Orgon, but that
progression comes to an abrupt halt in line 184. There is no
series, no logically necessary passage from one element to another,
but a heaping of signs on the portrait-sign. The besotted Orgon
calls Tartuffe his brother, loves him more than his own mother,
wife, or children, confides in him, asks his advice on his every
act, coddles and embraces him, stuffs him with the finest food,
and blesses him when he burps. As though the heap were complete, Dorine summarizes and catalogues: "Enfin il en est fou;
c'est son tout, son héros" (195). But not content with her summary, she surrounds it with still more signs: Orgon wonders at
Tartuffe, quotes him, sees his gestures as miraculous and his
words as oracular. The portrait seems to have been replaced by
cinema; and any comic pretense of logical necessity, by passion.
As the similar yet distinct frames race by us, Dorine's feelings

about Orgon's idolatry and its object become increasingly clear, and, by the time she reaches the servant Laurent, she is indulging in barely restrained name-calling ("fat" [203]; "traître" [207]).

Dorine's progression from portrait to description marks an attempt to pass in the text (and specifically in the family's means of dealing with the Orgon-Tartuffe crisis) from sign to rhetoric, from name to judgment, from designation to discourse. However representative or illusory the portraits, and in spite of the fact that they have successfully silenced Mme Pernelle, they have failed in their appointed task, that is, to clearly establish Tartuffe's identity for those who refuse to see it. Discourse, on the other hand, retains the power to both attribute names to things, and, in those names and in their relationship to verbs, to name essences, to judge. It not only signifies something, it also binds signs together with verbs of being, designating and encapsulating its own signs with additional ones, just as Dorine encircles the besotted Orgon with synonymous attributes or secondary signs (the words and gestures he addresses to Tartuffe). In the mouth of a more sophisticated speaker, these carefully ordered secondary signs become figures, the differed presence of the original sign — in short, the rhetorical apparatus.

It is Cléante, in scene v, Act I, who, confronted with Orgon, first undertakes to persuade through discourse, providing both a counterpoint to and completion of Dorine's role and the portraits. The moot point in the Orgon-Cléante debate remains the same as the object of the previous portrait debate, but this time it is stated explicitly:

> Vous ne connaissez pas celui dont vous parlez.
> [I. v. 267]

> Je ne le connais pas, puisque vous le voulez [268]

> Mon frère, vous seriez charmé de le connaître [270]

Orgon and Cléante both wish to establish certain knowledge of Tartuffe's identity and to persuade the other of their truth. As for Orgon, he entirely corroborates Dorine's portrait of him by his stated transformation (275) and unconditional surrender to his guest's somewhat shocking method of basic training. Unable to portray Tartuffe ("un homme...un homme enfin"), he dwells on the only element of their relationship that truly concerns him, that is, the degree to which the impostor fills his dual need to en-

49

slave and to obey, the attitude Jacques Guicharnaud calls a "mentalité de sous-officier ou de caporal."[23] Tartuffe is the Heaven-authorized guarantee Orgon needs to torture Mariane and the family in general, so that the moment he exceeds that specific function — in his purely autonomous bid for Elmire — marks the collapse of an empire for Orgon.

In a manner not unlike Dorine's, Orgon compiles a highly repetitive, sometimes descriptive, always emphatic restatement of his own sentiments. The information he provides in seven lines in fact reduces itself to two:

> Qui suit bien ses leçons goûte une paix profonde,
> Et comme du fumier regarde tout le monde. [I. v. 273–74]

Line 275 is a repetition of 273, the "Qui" replaced by "je," while lines 276–79 ("n'avoir affection pour rien," "De toutes amitiés il détache mon âme," "je verrais mourir frère, enfants . . .," "je m'en soucierais autant que de cela") provide accumulated synonyms for line 274 and for each other. While his remarks bear little resemblance to the portraits, he has hardly gone beyond Dorine's peculiarly static method of arguing.

If we must assume, in the case of a servant, that a lack of education and fixed class distinctions preclude logical, serial exposition, in Orgon's case the reasons are clearly indicated to be entirely other. Describing Tartuffe's spectacular performance in the church where they first met (281–310), Orgon states an epistemological preference. He is not interested in meaning as his age defines it, in the relationship between a sign and its own signified. For him there is no need to examine the necessity or arbitrariness of that bond, nor the one between subject and attribute. Knowledge for him is not that field in which signs must take root, nor language the translation or linear analysis of immediate, evident perceptions. Orgon is ridiculous precisely because he *equates* knowledge and perceptions. Faces and masks, sincerity and artifice, truth and appearance, currency and counterfeit are differences not identities, argues Cléante (331–38). But Orgon remains the ecstatic victim of one ultimately foolish judgment which, in seventeenth-century terms, would dangerously subvert knowledge, destroying language in the process. He dwells in the abyss of the proposition, "Knowing is seeing," a proposition which for everyone oppressed by it in the play cancels out its own first term.

Impossible copula from which Orgon draws his life force. With it he creates and controls Tartuffe's meaning, serves his creation, and cruelly dominates his family. While he will probably survive Tartuffe's betrayal, the latter's assertion of difference or separate and autonomous identity with himself, Orgon could not withstand the demonstration of that impossibility. The only means at the family's disposal of successfully resolving the crisis is to lure Tartuffe into the categories established by Orgon's outrageous judgment, with Elmire as bait. Elmire, the infinitely wise heroine of the play, seeks only to resolve a particular dilemma, not to shake the foundations of her spouse's being. It is she who most clearly delimits the family's task, diverting attention from Orgon's poor judgment to plans for outwitting Tartuffe. Whatever her motives, and even if she were willing to challenge the premise responsible for this particular crisis, such questioning would be tantamount to a request for suicide in theatrical terms, for any generalizing of Orgon's mistake about Tartuffe into an error concerning the way he knows the world would rob the former of a much more vital habitat than the one the impostor attempts to commandeer in Act V. He cannot afford to allow anyone to transform that impossible "is" into an "is not"; the resulting negation would destroy his shelter and the table at which he receives the nourishment necessary for him to survive as a thinking, speaking animal. In Cartesian terms, it would negate his certainty of existing. In Molière's terms, it would simply wipe him off the slate or stage.

Such is nevertheless Cléante's intention in Act I. Like the Port-Royal texts, his efforts are essentially corrective and constitute a lesson in contemporary logic. He opens with a statement of Orgon's blindness:

Voilà de vos pareils le discours ordinaire:
Ils veulent que chacun soit aveugle comme eux. [I. v. 318–19]

as opposed to his own clear-sightedness:

C'est être libertin que d'avoir de bons yeux [320]

His subsequent remarks, however, concern less Orgon's perceptions than the judgments he makes about them. He does not, like Elmire and even Dorine, attempt to demonstrate a coincidental blurring of vision where Tartuffe is concerned, but attacks Orgon's manner of knowing the world. Fully aware that Orgon's

51

fundamental proposition is an equation and that its terms are thus reversible, he prefaces his demonstration with a categorical refutation of the more accessible of its two possible forms:

> Les bons et vrais dévots, qu'on doit suivre à la trace,
> Ne sont pas ceux aussi qui font tant de grimace. [329–30]

Seeing is not knowing. We cannot know a man's nature by his gestures or the noises he makes. In fact, according to Cléante, the more pronounced the signs, the more likely they are to be deliberately deceitful, and the less certain the bond with the duly prescribed signified: "L'attention étant ainsi détournée du sens de la mimique à la mimique elle-même, si on tente de revenir à la chose imitée, on se trouve en face non plus de ce que la mimique visait à reproduire, mais de son contraire ou du moins, de son absence."[24] True signs are characterized by a certain plenitude, for they must contain a given signified, the one agreed upon in the lexicon of social intercourse. Those which fire Orgon's passion are, on the contrary, either empty or monstrously hybrid, as when Tartuffe's apparent humility in the face of Damis's accusations is bound to be a probable feeling of power and victory. Thus Orgon's initial judgment, or rather his equating of a perception translated into words with a judgment of it, is faulty.

Having erased that fault and thus cleared the ground for his own text, Cléante quickly brings on the "plat de résistance," the one most poisonous for Orgon, and repeatedly emphasizes its qualities for his understandably unenthusiastic interlocutor:

> . . . vous ne ferez nulle distinction
> Entre l'hypocrisie et la dévotion?
> Vous les voulez traiter d'un semblable langage,
> Et rendre même honneur au masque qu'au visage,
> Egaler l'artifice à la sincérité,
> Confondre l'apparence avec la vérité,
> Estimer le fantôme autant que la personne,
> Et la fausse monnaie à l'égal de la bonne? [331–38]

In a sense, Cléante unwittingly assures Orgon's deafness in the first lines of his exposition. Truth, and therefore truthful language or valid currency, cannot exist without the skillful discerning of difference, he says. Language is a game of oppositions before it is the dwelling place of identities, and one cannot recognize a legal coin without knowing what a false coin looks like.

Posing differentiation as a necessary prerequisite for comparison, as well as for the establishing of sameness, to a man whose existence depends upon the proposition that sameness is sameness automatically precludes the possibility of winning him over. It would not be illogical to play this scene with an Orgon entirely preoccupied with his fingernails, the window shades, or the door, for the very act of listening might seem threatening to him.

In this light Orgon's rather defensive interruption, a sarcastic recognition of extensive knowledge and profound wisdom, seems altogether apropos. But Cléante will not be diverted; he only uses the interruption to re-emphasize his point and the status he feels is his:

> . . . en un mot, je sais, pour toute ma science,
> Du faux avec le vrai faire la différence. [353–54]

Once his first principle and primary judgment is established in opposition to Orgon's own intuition, he offers an example of comparison by differentiation, illustrating his point even as he follows the method proposed. This portion of his tirade is divided almost exactly in half, an equilibrium he uses not to state an equation but to negate one, to run a slash through Orgon's equal sign. Lines 359 through 380 contain a thoroughly general commentary on falsely pious men, Tartuffe's specificity having fallen by the wayside. His central theme and strongest objection characterize themselves in images of public display, images heavily suggestive of the preparation and execution of a theatrical performance.

Theater would indeed seem an archetype of the hybrid sign, that fraudulent semiotic mutation whose existence is implied in Cléante's commentary on ostentatious piety. The "francs charlatans" of whom he speaks in line 361 are professional actors. They wear make-up and masks ("le dehors plâtré d'un zèle spécieux"), select a stage ("ces dévots de place"), contrive gestures ("trompeuse grimace," "faux clins d'yeux," "élans affectés"), and expect financial remuneration ("Font de dévotion métier et marchandise," "acheter crédit et dignités"). This comparison, like the larger comparison Cléante is drawing, rests, however, on a fundamental distinction, this one implicit. Theater and feigned religious zeal must be differentiated in the same way as good and bad faith. Theatrical artifice is not secret; Molière never asks his audience to interpret the people and situations he reproduces on stage as original presences equivalent to similar ones they meet outside the theater. His pretense remains an open imposture to which he asks the spectator to agree for a limited period of time. The King's decision to approve the play must ultimately come from his belief in that openness — that is, in Molière's good faith — and only from there. Impostors, on the other hand, do not warn us of their conversion of the world into a stage. There is no contract, no opportunity for a listener to opt for the spectator role or reject it. He simply assumes that he is participating in normal social intercourse, and by that very assumption, falls prey to the impostor.

As quietly implicit as Cléante's bona fide holy men, the difficult differentiation between good and bad faith is crucial, for on it hangs this play and Molière's defense of it. Truth and appearance, devotion and hypocrisy, faces and masks, coin and counterfeit are all necessarily determined by the integrity of whoever transmits them as signs, so that the only evidence on which a receiver can base his acceptance or rejection of these signs are his own impressions of the sender. The question, "Who is speaking?", necessarily precedes our faith in or skepticism about our interlocutor. Orgon is all the more ridiculous in that Tartuffe's performance is so poor that his bad faith and underlying nature should be evident, but Louis XIV can hardly be seen in the same light. There are at least plausible reasons for doubting Molière's texts and personal appeals, given the complex courtly intrigue that led to the condemnation of *Tartuffe*. A possible solution for the playwright, and one he clearly invoked at times, was to prove his identity as an honest man to Louis XIV, to foster the monarch's trust in him so that his words might be accepted on his word, his plays associated with the sincerity of his nature. It would thus not be unreasonable to hear an echo of the playwright-monarch relationship in Cléante's criteria for judging people and what they say. While I would hardly argue for an implicit "message" to Louis XIV in these lines, they do emphasize the ambiguity of the commentary on judgment in the Preface and in the play.

Descartes and the Port-Royal texts require a clear, self-evident intuition as a basis for logical deduction and a point of departure for the search for truth. Molière, on the other hand, treats of people more than of things, requiring knowledge of another person's nature for accurate interpretation of his words. And, as the Tartuffes of this world are a relatively rare species, judging good or bad faith is often a difficult matter, in spite of

54

Cléante's belief that "De ce faux caractère on en voit trop paraître" (381).

Cléante, however, is a man of principles even, and perhaps especially, where people are concerned. When he labels his ability to distinguish between faces and masks, a "science" he means it. He is not simply invoking a conventional metaphor, but like Dorine, suggests a comic image of the Cartesian method applied, or rather misapplied. He is the resident propounder of *Principia hominis*, a philosopher-scientist who prefers the *salon* to geometry. Using the implicit assumption of clear and evident bad faith, he deduces viciousness from vice, whence the surprising leap in line 374 from false piety to a hunger for revenge:

> Qui savent ajuster leur zèle avec leurs vices,
> Sont prompts, vindicatifs, sans foi, pleins d'artifices [373–74]

Viewed retrospectively, this passage of course becomes a foreshadowing of Tartuffe's speech at the end of Act IV:

> La maison m'appartient, je le ferai connaître,
> Et vous montrerai bien qu'en vain on a recours,
> Pour me chercher querelle, à ces lâches détours,
> Qu'on n'est pas où l'on pense en me faisant injure
> [IV. vii. 1558–61]

Cléante's grim vocabulary — "perdre quelqu'un," "fier ressentiment," "âpre colère," "nous assassiner" — should constitute a warning to Orgon and to the audience, but at this point in the play the danger is about as apparent as the logic in the jump from deceitful role-playing to vindictiveness.

The fact is that, in attempting to negate Orgon's equation, Cléante has created one of his own, an archetypal example of comparison by sameness. While he easily perceives the truth of Tartuffe's nature, on the general level at which he is speaking, his judgment is no more sound than Orgon's, for he deals in tautologies. He states a need for methodical discernment and differentiation with an example of difference (between impostors and saints), making method both the signifier and signified of his argument. If he wishes to identify difference, by his own rule he must begin with something different from difference — that is, sameness — then go on to truth or identity, lest his comparison cancel itself out, as in fact it does. If he had first equated the impostors described in lines 359–80 with the holy men described in lines 381–402 and *then* differentiated them, the difference between faulty and sound judgment would be clear. As it stands, his demonstration simply states that saints and impostors are different because they are different, the implied "Can-you-not-see,-Orgon?" adding only pomposity to his logic. He demonstrates not that he is right when he judges "y" and wrong when he judges "z," but that Orgon is wrong because he, Cléante is right, and thus that he is right because he is right. Similarly, assuming that vindictiveness necessarily accompanies dishonesty, then hypocrites inevitably seek revenge, which is to say that they are inevitably hypocrites.

Cléante's signifiers point only to themselves, for they are their own signified. Describing truly pious men, he says that they too are self-evident, that they are they:

De ce faux caractère on en voit trop paraître;
Mais les dévots de cœur sont aisés à connaître. [381–82]

The "mais" is deceptive, for there is little contrast between the two lines or between Cléante's means of recognizing truth and fraud. Ariston, Périandre, Oronte, etc., are sincerely devout men because they are not like Tartuffe. When he characterizes them, he finds himself limited to the negative: they do not do all the things hypocrites do, which things are by definition hypocritical. Instead of establishing a logical series, which would require signs pointing to other signs, Cléante has drawn a circle. While the representativeness of signs depends upon their ability to double back on themselves, this reflexive quality must be coupled with a pointing outward. Without that fundamental duality, unless they are *both* "indication" and "apparaître," signs are devoid of any representative power. In the same way, sound judgment requires both comparison and contrast, whereas Cléante's argument is based entirely on contrast. The result is a demonstration that Orgon should simply believe in him and view the world with his eyes because they are sharp. He does not show logical necessity but proposes himself as a model, adopting a stance that might describe the precise opposite of that which is carefully outlined in the *Discourse on Method*:

Voilà mes gens, voilà comme il en faut user,
Voilà l'exemple enfin qu'il se faut proposer. [403–04]

Jamais mon dessein ne s'est étendu plus avant que de tâcher à réformer mes propres pensées, et de bâtir dans

56

un fonds qui est tout à moi. Que si, mon ouvrage
m'ayant assez plu, je vous en fais voir ici le modèle, ce
n'est pas pour cela que je veuille conseiller à personne de
l'imiter.[25]

Cléante proposes himself as the unique model to be reproduced,
while Descartes suggests a possibility among possibilities, one
man's intellectual itinerary. Scientific method offers not truth
but a means of arriving at it, and Descartes is careful throughout
his work never to preclude other equally valid means.

*Tartuffe*, on the other hand, offers a truth at which no one seems
able to arrive. Everyone knows it by immediate perception, but
no one can demonstrate it to Orgon. In the end, Cléante did not
succeed any more than Dorine in transcending a claim to superior
eyesight and so was never able to construct a logical series either
to or from the perception of which everyone wishes to convince
Orgon. Tartuffe himself will have to appear and surrender the
key, an alternative to the family's obstinate desire to correct
Orgon's vision and thus his judgment, since the two correspond
in his case. He does so in Act III, inspiring in Elmire the idea of
abandoning the search for corrective lenses in favor of a simple
modification in what appears before Orgon's eyes. She cannot
correct her husband's visual disorder, but she can alter the road
signs and thus momentarily restore order in the house.

Tartuffe, like the others, must enter into the order of things
and signs; his behavior must illustrate his portrait so that the sign
may be successfully rehabilitated in a reunion with its proper
signified. He is both double and duplicitous, and because his enterprise depends upon the bisecting of what in an orderly social
and linguistic universe constitutes a whole, the havoc he wreaks
manifests itself as crippling disunion. This halving process — of
signified from sign, of Mariane from Valère, Elmire from Orgon,
Orgon from his son, and finally, the family corpus from its physical and financial environment — renders powerless each of the
isolated parts, forcing them into morally reprehensible functions
not unlike the impostor's own role. Under Tartuffe's reign, signs
would propagate lies; Mariane would be unfaithful to him and
Elmire to Orgon; Damis would be in danger of becoming a disinherited vagabond and the family would suffer a total disgrace,
its fortune probably consecrated to further wrong-doing. Were
he successful, no one and nothing could function in accordance

with its duly-appointed "nature"; all would be dislocated and hybrid in a clumsily pasted world of the "comme si,"[26] an ongoing apocalypse of knowledge, language, and society. In this sense, the royal intervention that closes the play seems entirely logical, for Tartuffe's attempt to create a world in his own image constitutes a real and present danger to the body politic.

Without the *communitas*, the divine monarch is powerless, just as, by the same principle, Satan's influence requires the isolation of formerly united elements. In a work he calls *Le Système des objets* (subtitled "La Consommation des signes"), Jean Baudrillard stresses the crucial link between family structures and the semiotics of physical environment:

> L'intérieur bourgeois type est d'ordre patriarcal: c'est l'ensemble salle à manger chambre à coucher. Les meubles, divers dans leur fonction, mais fortement intégrés, gravitent autour du buffet ou du lit de milieu. . . . Les meubles se regardent, se gênent, s'impliquent dans une unité qui est moins spatiale que d'ordre moral. Ils s'ordonnent autour d'un axe qui assure la chronologie régulière des conduites: la présence toujours symbolisée de la famille à elle-même. . . . chaque meuble, chaque pièce à son tour intériorise sa fonction et en revêt la dignité symbolique — la maison entière parachevant l'intégration des relations personnelles dans le groupe semi-clos de la famille.
>
> Tout ceci compose un organisme dont la structure est la relation patriarcale de tradition et d'autorité et dont le cœur est la relation affective complexe qui lie tous ses membres.[27]

The furniture Tartuffe would have removed from the house in the final scene of the play constitutes an ordered system of signs. On a symbolic level, were he to succeed in forcing the buffet and the bed out into the street, that system would no longer have a center, for Orgon's authority as father and head-of-household would be dissolved, and the context of his relationship with each family member and with the group as a whole, destroyed. The removal of each additional piece of furniture would similarly terminate every member's role in the system, leaving them with no leader and no basis on which to relate to one another. By leveling the hierarchy, Tartuffe would consecrate his final victory over Orgon: once enslaved by the latter's power to create and perpetuate his identity, he would now not only have liberated himself (seducing Elmire would suffice for that), but could act as master. The situation would have exactly reversed itself. Orgon the poverty-stricken, disgraced subject would have become Tartuffe's destruction / creation, as much a "lie" as his own obligatory piety, and he would be free to introduce his subversive system of nonsigns into his former master's house. It is as though, the page having been appropriated by Tartuffe, the letters lay in a senseless heap on the floor. The jumble of furniture in the street finishes Orgon, but it also inflicts chaos on the common domain.

Victorious, Tartuffe would constitute a public menace. That page and his dwelling belong to a larger system and, controlled by him, endanger that system by their apparent conformity to it. He is in a position to represent himself as a good citizen and loyal patriot, as a group member like any other, while consuming people and things at the expense of the community and rendering every disservice to the King. The antilanguage on the page is also antisocial, for Tartuffe alone controls its meaning, although the community reads it, and into it communally accepted signs. His habitat resembles any other, but houses no hierarchical system of exchange patterned on the political order, only a system whose form and content reduce themselves to one man. Just as the family unit splits and reaches a crisis state because of Tartuffe's insatiable appetite — for food, for the security Mariane represents, for Elmire, and then for a fortune — and because of the leader's blindness, so will the community be divided against itself if it allows Tartuffe to remain within it as a contributing patriotic member of the body politic. The contemporary concept of order remains absolute: it requires a logical chain in which every link must be certain. No member of a hierarchy can function both as him- or herself and as his or her opposite without danger to the entire system.

It is by vaunting his ability to sabotage semiotic systems that Tartuffe reveals the source of his power to Elmire, thus rendering it vulnerable. Only Louis XIV can resolve the essentially political problem of the incriminating documents and of the family's relationship to society, but in Act III Elmire is at least empowered with a means of repairing severed ties within the family. It is not as though the nature of Tartuffe's bid surprises her: both his insatiable appetite and lack of scruples are by now entirely familiar, and if she has considered the possibility of this particular manifestation of his hunger, there has surely been no question in her mind as to the feasibility of just such a declaration. In any case, it could hardly seem incongruous to her, as she would indicate in line 962. Her surprise must refer more to the time and place, then, and perhaps to some indignation on her part, than to the event itself. She is also seeking to check the snowball effect of his speech, for she has good reason at this point to wish to prevent him from reintegrating his own identity (and, by the same token, repairing his ability to *represent* that self), thus attaining his autonomy vis-à-vis Orgon. What she learns in scene iii, however, is precisely that Tartuffe has subjected himself to a kind of deliberate self-mutilation in order to feed his ever-growing appetite and, to keep pace with his hunger, fully intends to inflict the same process on her and on others.

Elmire realizes that the bargain she imposes at the end of the scene is scarcely one for Tartuffe. While it assures a continued flow of nourishment, it checks the expansion of that flow, thus protecting the family from possible inanition, but limiting Tartuffe to a diet that is no longer sufficient. Such is precisely her intention. Powerless to evict him from the premises, she must nevertheless reduce his strength and prevent him from utilizing the tactics he reveals to her.

His very salutation bisects her being, perhaps through convention, but also because of personal preference:

Que le Ciel à jamais par sa toute bonté
Et de l'âme et du corps vous donne la santé [III. iii. 879–80]

The distinction is an altogether convenient one for him and announces his promise to leave at least part of Elmire untarnished:

Votre honneur avec moi ne court point de hasard,
Et n'a nulle disgrâce à craindre de ma part. [987–88]

Unlike her body, Elmire's honor will remain pure. No one need know of their liaison; Elmire's reputation will not be endangered. That is, others will "read" her exactly as before; they will interpret her words and gestures and make judgments about her true nature or "content" as they always have. At the same time, her physical person will be free to indulge independently in pleasures which the same people would consider morally reprehensible. Apart from the fact that husbands like Tartuffe have already been described in Act II as excellent reasons for wifely infidelity, there is nothing in the text to indicate that Elmire, an "honnête femme," could live with the reprobate body to whose revel Tartuffe alludes ("amour sans scandale," "plaisir sans peur"), that she could ever in any sense make it her own. He is proposing a rape of her integrity in the broadest sense of the word, a violation of her wholeness as a person, combined with a clandestine modification of her identity which would render her a stranger unto herself and to others.

This severing of body from honor and the grafting onto the latter of a totally foreign mass suggests a fundamentally threatening, if comic, disruption of the order of the epistemological universe common to many forms of Western literature — Dr. Frankenstein busily transferring brains to surgically reconstructed bodies in his basement laboratory. Tartuffe wishes to recreate Elmire, just as Orgon has reassembled him, from disparate elements. And as in the Frankenstein myth, the result of such meddling in divine prerogatives can only be evil. The specious reconciliation of Heaven and earth with which Tartuffe attempts to seduce Elmire cannot work because it is *not* a reconciliation but the sleight-of-hand triumph of worldly desire:

> Mais enfin je connus, ô beauté toute aimable,
> Que cette passion peut n'être point coupable,
> Que je puis l'ajuster avecque la pudeur,
> Et c'est ce qui m'y fait abandonner mon cœur. [949–52]

A mysterious adjustment that resembles more a tinkering with categories than the creation of one into which adultery would readily fit.

Tartuffe, the clandestine mutilator of systems, foreshadows Dom Juan, the manifest creator of a new one. His "interchangeable parts" attitude toward people aims at the endless satisfaction of boundless desire, a mutated Eden fit for and controlled by fallen man. Tartuffe seeks not the peace and harmony of fulfillment, but to piece together an earthly paradise in which he might release his hunger from all restriction, thus assuring its continued existence. Tartuffe *is* his appetite and can only regain his integrity by liberating that desire, using reverse surgery to reunite his meaning with the signs prescribed by order. Thus he is "sincere" in his bid for Elmire; speaking in accordance with his nature, he becomes momentarily whole and free, free of the hideous graft that is his piety.

Unfortunately, that liberation, like the willful enslavement that preceded it, must remain a secret, for the unqualified sign "desire" is incompatible with any seventeenth-century system.[28] Tartuffe does not fit in anywhere. Even structured like other signs, he cannot function with them, for, apocalyptic by definition, his signified consumes all others. Like a word whose presence on the page requires the erasing of entire sentences and paragraphs, he is too thoroughly imprisoned in his own nature to participate in a hierarchical order, in an analytical enumeration or logical progression. He cannot live in Orgon's household without destroying it. Whether natural or mutated, orderly or subversive, he remains an outlaw sign in a semiotic universe based on the rigidly binary principle that sameness requires the identification and "systematic" exclusion of difference. Whatever the order, it must remain absolute or dissolve. Except on stage, declares Molière from the stage — at once defending and illustrating the moral utility of his craft — healthy organisms cannot tolerate a single parasite, society a single criminal, logic a single error, representation a single illusion. Relative to any system of signs, Tartuffe is different and therefore mortally dangerous. His only hope for survival is to enter some network incognito, turn it upside down, devour it, and hope that the *Ius* (Orgon, Louis XIV) will smile upon him for having eliminated chaos from the world.

Because the disguise he must wear in order to please Orgon suits him so poorly, Tartuffe's position in the house is tenuous at the outset, a factor he fails to take into account with Elmire. Whether we speak of people or furniture, each sign in a system defines and describes the others. We can analyze the network into units, but they have little importance for us except in relation to each other. Damis may be a colorful fellow, but we are only interested in him as Orgon's son. Dorine provokes particularly amusing scenes because she is a family servant; Elmire could not foil Tartuffe were she not Orgon's wife; and Orgon himself would surely mean nothing to us were it not for his failings as a husband and father and his passion for Tartuffe. Each sign both manifests itself and says something about the others. The latter would be impossible without the former, but it is the indication of other signs which moves the text, providing meaning and a story.

Because of the considerable ambiguity inherent in a signified which functions not only as half of a sign but as an exterior referent — an ambiguity that pervades both the Port-Royal texts and the relationship between truth and logic in Cartesian epistemology — reality and people's real natures at the same time are and are not important. Neither can exist except by virtue of the other in a system of discourse, yet human nature also exists as a thing in the world, that to which we refer a character's behavior in order to verify its "sincerity." Meaning is both a strictly binary play — from signifier to signified, from sign to sign — and requires a third referential quality. Paradoxically, this quality comes from the real world at the same time that it remains entirely inscribed in the signified or in the relationship between two signs. It is precisely that ambiguity which Tartuffe lacks, and that lack divests him of representational power. He is himself only, a perfectly clear nature with no mysterious tie to anything or anyone else in the universe of the play. He is not equivocal but hypocritical, outside the linguistic system altogether. Entirely alone, he suffers the senselessness of tautology.[29] He can manifest himself, as he does with Elmire, but that very manifestation precludes any interdependent relationship. He can enter the text only by a process of misrepresentation, thus establishing an ersatz meaning in relation to Orgon, who cannot afford to realize that Tartuffe lacks the equipment to secure any exterior ties. However, in this case "misrepresentation" involves more than a simple substitution of one identity for another. Tartuffe acts as though he possessed representational powers incompatible with his nature: his relationships with God and with Orgon could not exist. There is no synonym for him; he is not Heaven's servant or Orgon's friend, but an appetite trying to act like a hypocrite trying to play a pious man. Like any other sign, he possesses indicative powers, but they are twisted back toward himself; he manifests himself as Tartuffe and indicates Tartuffe. One would have to be as semiologically confused as Orgon to accept his clumsy poses as representative.

Elmire, on the other hand, is a good actress capable of recognizing similar talent, or the lack of it, in others. She not only is herself; she also quite successfully plays Orgon's wife, Mme Pernelle's daughter-in-law, and Damis's and Mariane's stepmother. Tartuffe's blunder with her can only be attributed to a total ignorance of her critical expertise or, another way of saying the same thing, to the all-encompassing fact of his hunger.

With Orgon, Tartuffe cannot be himself even when he is;

with Elmire and the others, he cannot help being himself even when he wishes not to be. Elmire knows him well and can hardly be expected to accept his promise:

> Mais les gens comme nous brûlent d'un feu discret,
> Avec qui pour toujours on est sûr du secret . . . [995–96]

Such may truly be his intention, but he is offering that which he has proven himself least capable of giving: a good performance, the convincing representation of a participant in a network of interrelationships. Since Elmire is not at all tempted, his lack of talent alone would not seem dangerous, but his *modus operandi* presents a distinct threat to everyone in the house.

Elmire can momentarily fend for herself by simply refusing Tartuffe, so that the only immediate danger is to Mariane, about to be "tartuffiée," as Dorine says. It is up to Elmire to prevent Tartuffe from forcing her stepdaughter into the role of an impostress. Cast as the loving and devoted wife of a man who disgusts her, Mariane will surely not survive. Except for Dorine, she would be altogether too willing to abandon comedy for the Phèdre-like role of a suicidal tragedienne. Thus Elmire invokes blackmail ("Je ne redirai point l'affaire à mon époux . . . presser tout franc . . . L'union de Valère avecque Mariane" [1015–18]) to prevent Tartuffe from inverting the family system and subverting its meaning, while allowing him to live in proximity with that system. He may stay if he relinquishes his demonic scalpel. Regardless of the long-range feasibility of such a solution, Tartuffe is momentarily foiled. Only Damis's intervention saves him and obliges Elmire to seek a more permanent solution, armed as she now is with a knowledge of Tartuffe's methods.

Damis's enterprise — ". . . détromper mon père, et luy mettre en plein jour / L'âme d'un scélérat . . ." (1027–28) — has already proven fruitless insofar as both Orgon and Mme Pernelle are concerned (Act I). Yet Damis continues to wish to establish the existence of a signified for someone who does not distinguish signifieds as separate entities. Like Tartuffe, Orgon is caught up in a tautology, for he can no more afford to discern the paradoxical same-otherness of the signified on which meaning depends than can his guest. He sees signifiers and signifieds as one and the same thing, with no referential quality involved. It is useless to talk about Tartuffe's "soul," because Orgon does not admit the possibility of its differing from the signs he displays and therefore cannot make judgments in either the Port-Royal or

Cartesian sense. Since he is entirely dependent upon perceptions, meaning does not exist for him. Secondly, even if Damis's enterprise were intelligible to Orgon, he would not accept the testimony of someone else's eyes. Perception is all he needs, but it must be his own, since he defines knowledge as immediate sensory stimulus. For him the incident Damis describes simply did not occur. What he perceives is a Tartuffe prepared to accept all charges on holy principle, and that remains the truth of the matter:

> De quelque grand forfait qu'on me puisse reprendre,
> Je n'ai garde d'avoir l'orgueil de m'en défendre. [1081–82]

Thanks to Orgon's poor eyes and ignorance of meaning, Tartuffe can perform his abominable plastic surgery on Damis. The somewhat rebellious but essentially loyal son must leave his father's house disinherited and disfigured. Delirious with power, driven by sadism, and frightened of losing Tartuffe, Orgon adopts the impostor, orders him to frequent Elmire, and accelerates plans for his wedding. With the system shattered and Tartuffe free to devour the pieces, Elmire must act.

Since Orgon remains so intensely enamored of appearances, Elmire offers him one, knowing he will convert it into a judgment. She does not tell him to see for himself, but proposes an active assault on his line of vision, with her as the aggressor:

> Si je vous faisais voir . . . [1340]

> De vous le faire voir . . . [1342]

> . . . vous fît clairement tout voir . . . [1346]

> . . . je vous fasse témoin [1352]

She makes of him a passive spectator by forcing upon Tartuffe the same operation he has performed on the others, but in reverse. She can thus right the people and relationships Tartuffe has turned upside down. If Orgon will consent to temporarily relinquish his position as ruler, she will show him he has lost that power and restore it to him. If she can lead the appetite into action, she will permanently strip it of its power to consume.

Thus Elmire accomplishes that demonstration of sameness via difference bungled by Cléante in Act I. Incapable of understanding that such is her purpose, Orgon becomes so engrossed in the process that he forgets the point, context, or meaning of events. A stranger to logical progression, he gives himself to immediate perception; ignorant of difference, he forgets that his passivity is only a means to an end and should convert to difference, to authority, at Elmire's signal. On the contrary, it will require an interruption of the performance and Tartuffe's temporary departure for him to abandon the spectator role, decode the signal, and reunite the signifiers (Tartuffe's behavior) with their now unavoidable signifieds (seducer, impostor, thief, traitor, etc.)

Nevertheless, Elmire has succeeded in putting the impostor back together. He now looks like a hypocrite, even to Orgon. If the latter cannot see that even hypocrisy is a poor act for an appetite trapped in itself, it is because he does not and never will comprehend the mechanism of representation. In a comic universe where human nature is an absolute given truth, Orgon cannot grow into intelligence capable of comprehending the subtleties of meaning. No matter, for this play. With a system of signs once again operative, Tartuffe's only remaining arm also threatens a more powerful warrior than he.

# Meaning in Transit:
# The Self-Destruct Mechanism

> C'est pourquoi la possession d'un objet quel qu'il
> soit est toujours si satisfaisante et si décevante à la
> fois: toute une série la prolonge et l'inquiète. C'est
> un peu la même chose sur le plan sexuel: si la rela-
> tion amoureuse vise l'être dans sa singularité, la pos-
> session amoureuse . . . ne se satisfait que d'une suc-
> cession d'objets ou de la répétition du même, ou de
> la supposition de tous les objets.
>
> — Jean Baudrillard[1]

If Tartuffe and Orgon dwell in the static universe of the copula,
Dom Juan and Sganarelle move in and through transitive verbs.
Tartuffe *is* his appetite; Dom Juan indulges his. The former, a
"déclassé" who cannot function in any system, is ineluctably and
inescapably himself; the latter chooses his strangely indefinable
conduct freely. A member of a highly privileged caste, Dom Juan
uses that membership to his every advantage but, eternally itiner-
ant, refuses any real participation in it; his relationship with
Sganarelle is defined in terms of that refusal and of the valet's
inability to comprehend it. His fall from the Olympian heights of
hedonism into the tortures of hell corresponds to events in or
prior to the play which trace a similar downward social spiral:
the progressively more difficult seductions of Elvire, a "jeune
fiancée," Charlotte and Mathurine, and, finally, the Poor Man,
whom he totally fails to seduce. At the bottom of the spiral his
free will begins to evaporate rapidly. It is not only that he chooses

to play Tartuffe's role after the events of Act IV; he has also been forced into it by a long succession of intruder-obstacles who will not allow him to satisfy an appetite sharpened by the day's exploits. Pierrot's untimely arrival prevented him from consummating his verbal seduction of Charlotte in Act II; Mathurine's entrance in scene iv of the same act precluded his enjoyment of either of the peasant women, and in the end, almost anyone, from the farcical M. Dimanche to his Corneillian father, can stop him from eating his dinner.

Immediately following, the Statue, an ambiguous but terrifying conglomerate sign / symbol suggestive of feminine ire, noble revenge, paternal malediction, and Divine Justice, returns the audience to heights beyond even the top of the spiral and obliges a Dom Juan relentlessly tracked by all the forces suggested to take cover. In adopting a mask, Dom Juan for the first time places himself in and at the service of a system of signs. It is this throwing of a bone, in the form of a false definition, back to the hunters that inspires Sganarelle's most comical, yet also his most poignant, expression of horror in Act V, scene ii, and kindles the fires of damnation around Dom Juan. From a thorn in everyone's side, he has become in Act V a concrete, readily identifiable threat to the verbal-societal-religious order, in the same way that Tartuffe constituted an immediate threat to the community and Louis XIV when he attempted to confiscate Orgon's house.

The difficulty one always encounters in attempting to discuss Dom Juan is that he and the play itself are entirely atypical in relation to the structures of both late seventeenth-century drama and contemporary sign theory. At the outset Dom Juan appears to be Tartuffe's precise opposite, but there ends any possibility of invoking or suggesting a state of being or definition in conjunction with his name. While we can describe and judge his behavior, he continues to defy both the other characters' and the critic's efforts to label him, at least until Act V. He refuses membership in, and therefore loyalty to, any social, linguistic, or religious order, whereas Tartuffe selects certain orders for consumption and infiltrates them disguised as an apparently loyal member. In the dinner scene (IV. vii) Dom Juan savors and moves on to the next course, while Sganarelle, like Tartuffe, seeks to devour everything in sight but is carried forward by his master's authority over him and over those serving the meal.

This sampling — of women, of foods, of systems, of signs — permeates Dom Juan's behavior throughout the play and locates him in a zone of nondefinition. His inconsistencies, although they can be and have been reconciled in various systems of critical discourse, nevertheless make of him a late eighteenth-century or early nineteenth-century romantic hero rather than a seventeenth-century comic stereotype. He seduces, marries, mistreats, saves, cheats, subsidizes, and deprives the objects he encounters in his travels. Unlike Tartuffe, he utilizes rather than devours, never depleting the resources or fulfilling the needs with which he comes into contact. At a general thematic level, his habitual transience can be easily inscribed in the "libertin de cour" tradition. His credo and sense of his own superhuman powers ("je me sens un cœur à aimer toute la terre; et comme Alexandre, je souhaiterais qu'il y eût d'autres mondes.") can and must be read in the same context with Francion's astrological sighs:

> . . . mon naturel n'a de l'inclination qu'au mouvement, je suis tousjours en une douce agitation . . .

> . . . je ne touche ce beau sein qu'en tremblant, mon souverain plaisir est de frétiller, je suis tout divin, je veux estre tousjours en mouvement comme le Ciel.[2]

However, while Francion and his comrades subscribe to a countercode in order to free themselves, Dom Juan refuses to indulge fully in any system, whence his option for genuinely marginal status and his arithmetical profession of faith to Sganarelle in Act III, scene i ("Je crois que deux et deux sont quatre"). Tartuffe desires entry into every system; Dom Juan remains quite content on the periphery, compiling his text with signs, signals, and indices borrowed from many systems, and will not be lured, wheedled, or forced into any until Act V. Unless we wish to see him as some sort of proponent of scientific rationalism, we must leave him undefined until that point and focus our attention on his behavior, specifically on the way in which he arranges and distributes signs.

His addiction to movement solicits discussion precisely because it cannot be ascribed simply to the libertine code of "générosité." In a context entirely different from my own, J. D. Hubert says of this play: "Whereas in previous plays the author had created characters who tend to substitute words and concepts for action and existence, in *Dom Juan* he makes speech itself a substitute for action."[3] In bringing discourse and action together, however, Molière has moved from a language of attribution to one of transition, and thus into a grammatical and logical mode conspicuously absent from seventeenth-century theoretical texts.

As I pointed out in Chapter 1, the Port-Royal *Grammar* divides the parts of speech into two categories: "les objets des pensées" and "la manière des pensées," the latter consisting of verbs, conjunctions, and interjections. The whole discussion is limited to and considered part and parcel of a theory of judgment or knowledge of things expounded in chapters 12 to 16 of the *Grammar*. Four years later, in a second edition, the authors of the *Logic* remained confident enough of the adequacy of these pages to simply reproduce chapter 13 of the *Grammar*, "Des Verbes: et ce qui leur est propre et essentiel," as their own chapter 2, Part II, "Du Verbe." The 1664 additions to the *Logic* demonstrate an even more stringent attitude in regard to the potential opacity of rhetoric than the previous edition. Whereas the maintenance of the natural clarity of language depends upon its transparence in relation to thought, figures often mask, deform, or erase what thought would elaborate, an attitude most clearly expressed in the "Second Preliminary Discourse":

> L'esprit fournit assez de pensées; l'usage donne les expressions; et pour les figures et les ornements, on n'en a toujours que trop. . . .

> . . . s'éloigner . . . d'un style artificiel et rhétoricien composé de pensées fausses et hyperboliques et de figures forcées qui est le plus grand de tous les vices.[4]

It is significant that the chapter on verb theory was in fact added to the *Logic* in 1664 and that it defines a verb as "un mot dont le principal usage est de signifier l'affirmation."[5] — that is, as a copula in a discourse of attribution or judgment:

> . . . le Verbe de lui-même ne devrait point avoir d'autre usage que de marquer la liaison que nous faisons dans notre esprit des deux termes d'une proposition. Mais il n'y a que le Verbe *être* qu'on appelle substantif, qui soit demeuré dans cette simplicité, et encore n'y est-il proprement demeuré que dans la troisième personne du présent *est*.[6]

70

While certain intransitive verbs are described as copula plus attribute ("Pierre vit" = "Pierre est vivant"), any consideration of transitive verbs as such is strictly excluded, an omission which invites our attention because of its particular relevance to the present reading of Molière. It is, of course, a question of the ideology inherent in the theory of representation prevalent in the latter half of the seventeenth century. For twenty-three years and in the course of four editions of the *Logic*, the problems of the structure of the sign, of the relationship between meaning and external reference, and of the verb's ambiguous status (affirmative act, link in a chain of representations, but also *articulation of things in the world*)[7] remained implicit. Then in a fifth edition that appeared in 1683, the authors openly confronted the problem of language, adding an ensemble of texts which treat those questions explicitly, thus bringing language to the forefront in a manual of logic.

Contemporary polemic between Port-Royal and certain Protestant ministers over the doctrine of transubstantiation provided the stimulus for that confrontation within the *Logic*. The statement "This is my body" constitutes the locus of an encounter between an act of language and logical reflection on language, between speech and linguistics. According to Catholic dogma, the copula possesses real ontological powers, for by simple affirmation it can accord being to a demonstrative pronoun, turning "this" not only into the predicate "body" but into the speaker's being. If "body" is read as a figure or metaphor, the distinction (difference) between things in the world and words in propositions remains clear, but the ambiguity of the referent, and therefore of the *relationship* between things and words, stands. If, on the other hand, the thing indicated by the neuter pronoun becomes, by the power invested in the verb "to be," the speaker's body, then Christ's affirmation constitutes a linguistic transubstantiation of words into things, a truly adequate articulation of the world. In the latter case, difference breaks down, but the problem of the referent is eliminated. If sign and signified are identical, there is no need for or possibility of exteriority of any kind.

The *Logic* seems to oscillate between the two conflicting yet simultaneous alternatives, between the necessity of logical rigor in order to establish a rational grammar and that of loyalty to the mystery of Catholic doctrine. While the Eucharist seems an extreme example and not in and of itself a crucial problem for human logic (the presence of a divine speaker renders the propo-

71

sition atypical in any case), it nevertheless typifies the central epistemological problem of seventeenth-century linguistics and clearly locates that problem in its ideological context. Thus, in 1683, the authors of the *Logic*, or *Art of Thinking*, brought certain theological debates into the domain of logic, suggesting a "natural" rapport between French classical norms and ideals and profound philosophical or religious convictions. Classical discourse strives for clarity just as men strive to be like Christ, whose discourse alone is perfectly adequate. In a culture whose ideology so concerns itself with the adequacy (and eventual correspondence) of words and things, where sameness becomes the ideal or goal of difference, the verb "to be" reigns absolute. It is at once a Louis XIV-like representation and a Christ-like incarnation. Correlatively, in a linguistic system which defines all propositions as affirmations or ontological judgments, transitive verbs are irrelevant. They have no theoretical value because, whatever their representative powers, they could never incarnate, but only go on describing. Like the portraits in *Tartuffe*, they may or may not represent, but they certainly do not represent the representativeness of representation.[8]

If someone were to suddenly insert a chapter on transitive verbs in a seventeenth-century *Grammar* or *Logic* or to include a series of cooking recipes in Descartes' *Meditations*, we would have an analogy for Dom Juan's relationship to the other characters in the play. He must not be irrelevant since he is there, they feel, but what could he possibly mean in any of the various contexts in which he sets up temporary residence? And what do his actions mean in relation to each other and to himself as a sign? How should we read this play in relation to Molière's others? It is not without reason that critics have so often accused the character Dom Juan and the play itself of incoherence, yet it is difficult to study the relationship of part to whole when we are dealing with such a recalcitrant part. In spite of Sganarelle's firm belief that he is an incarnation of evil, Dom Juan is simply not available for participation in the great moral and philosophical dramas of his time, whence his silence at certain crucial moments in the play. He has no interest either in the truths established by an ideology or in their opposites. Until Act V he does not, like Tartuffe, concern himself with natural and artificial meanings nor with the appropriation of language and culture and the threat of humiliating regression to a primitive state which so preoccupy Arnolphe. In Act II he appears totally unabashed by the fiasco in which his seafaring kidnap plans have resulted, and equally so by the necessity of standing naked before a peasant's fire. While Elvire's inappropriate costume in Act I, scene iii, irritates him, his own display of signs and symbols and his relationship to context remain fairly unimportant. He is vain, but clearly does not view his clothing as a sign of linguistic acculturation as does Arnolphe, nor does he consider the individual items Pierrot so carefully enumerates as minimal units of signification constituting the judgment: "Il faut que ce soit queuque gros, gros Monsieur" (II. i). He thinks not in terms of what is but of what happens; he perplexes and dismays everyone because they insist on reading him, and that in the context of a system. For them it is a question either of who they think he is (Sganarelle, Pierrot) or of whom they want him to be (Elvire, Dom Louis) — that is, of his clarity and usefulness as an integral and integrated sign, and, on another level, of his goodness or evil. For him it is a question of "two and two are four."

Dom Juan's unavailability for the game of meaning in which everyone attempts to discover his role or to assign him one forms a basis for the freedom of action to which he aspires. It permits him to indulge his impetuous appetite as he moves in and out of various systems of signs — social classes, marriage and interpersonal relationships in general, clothes — and especially of language itself. There are two principal methods that Dom Juan employs to withdraw to the periphery of language, each of which has the effect of either stopping all theoretical discussion — of identity, morals, or knowledge — and bringing it around to his favorite subject, his plans for the next seduction, or drawing out his interlocutor in such a way as to force him or her to flounder in a self-revealing monologue. The first of these is a kind of interrogation which obliges the other to broach a subject he, Dom Juan, has chosen with a view to absenting himself in order to avoid establishing any personal identity until the other has been rendered totally vulnerable to his subsequent attack on affirmative judgment (i.e. the whole range of possible objections to his conduct).

It is thus that he first appears to us in Act I. His first eight speeches consist of nine questions about Elvire's squire, Gusman, and how Sganarelle handled him, but he seems less interested in Sganarelle's individual replies than in maneuvering his valet into initiating a conversation about his own amorous adventures. What he wants is not to know who Gusman is, but to act, to plan his next seduction, whence, paradoxically, his question: ". . . quelle est ta pensée là-dessus?" (I. ii), which leads Sganarelle directly into a trap. Although he certainly does not have at his fingertips the clear knowledge of Dom Juan to which he lays claim, Sganarelle has learned what to *do* to please his master and thus escape the physical punishment the latter would readily inflict. He immediately senses that Dom Juan wishes to talk about transitions — that is, the next lady to be conquered — and obliges only too willingly with images of movement ("le plus grand coureur du monde," "se promener," "n'aime guère demeurer . . ."). However, there is implicit disapproval in his appeasement, for he says "se promener *de liens en liens*" and "demeurer *en place*" (my italics), suggesting something slightly illicit about so many broken ties and an inability to keep still even for a while. "Liens" and "demeurer en place" are proper norms which, in Sganarelle's eyes, Dom Juan wrongly refuses to accept. The latter has only to render explicit this implicit affirmation in order to demolish it. He hints at his nihilistic enterprise even as he prepares his attack, but the valet, who functions as a loyal member of a system based on ontological affirmation, can no longer escape: "Et *ne* trouves-tu *pas*, dis moi, que j'ai raison d'en user de la sorte?" (I. ii; my italics). Neither a question nor a statement, the negative interrogative comfortably locates Dom Juan on a periphery from which he can destroy Sganarelle and at which he attains an immunity to his valet's objections simply because he is not participating in the same binary system. From a linguistic point of view, Sganarelle has only affirmations and negations at his disposal: he must either say something *is* or *is not*. From a moral standpoint, he can speak only in terms of right and wrong: Dom Juan either is or is not justified. The master, on the other hand, has all the room he needs to collect the requisite signs for constructing a reply altogether outside that system of binary options, a totally nihilistic discourse which, like the absurdity of a cooking recipe tacked on to Descartes' *Principles of Philosophy*, destroys all unity of affirmation. "Eh! Monsieur," groans the valet, feeling understandably discomfited.

Sganarelle cannot help comprehending that the key to Dom Juan's conduct is his will, and so, when commanded to speak, he acquiesces in a desperate attempt to get out of his predicament: ". . . vous avez raison, si vous le voulez . . . Mais si vous ne le vouliez pas, ce serait peut-être une autre affaire" (I. ii). What he fails to understand is that that will, unlike Arnolphe's, remains free, in the sense of *absolute*; Dom Juan does not want a "yes" or a "no"; he wants Sganarelle to do (or, here, to *say*, as Hubert points out) what he wants him to do, so that he, Dom Juan, can do (say) as he pleases. Arnolphe uses direct force to oblige people to stop talking and do his bidding ("je parle: allez, obéissez"), while Dom Juan invokes the imperative "parle" as a preparatory measure for obtaining what he really wants, which remains unspecified.

He begins with a familiar ironic style, assuming the Socratic pretense of ignorance and of willingness to learn (from Sganarelle). However, whereas in the Socratic method adroit questioning is employed in order to render conspicuous the other's false conceptions, Dom Juan uses it not to negate specific notions but to eliminate Sganarelle's whole frame of reference, his semiotic universe, to replace definition with a preference for movement and change. He initiates a chain of events in a familiar and conventional ironic mode, but arrives at a result so totally incongruous with the normal or expected mode that he has moved to a second degree of irony by ironizing Socratic irony. That, in turn, will be subject to irony, when in his monologue he begins to borrow signs from Sganarelle's own repertoire in order to express something other than their accepted meaning. It is thus perpetually unclear to Sganarelle precisely what Dom Juan is expressing or wills, since he continually moves on to further degrees of irony, undermining the very possibility of meaning in contemporary terms — a stasis, a subject attributed with some quality via the verb "to be." When he accords freedom of speech to his valet, it is not ultimately to learn his opinion, as he says: ". . . je te donne la liberté de parler et de me dire tes sentiments" (I. ii), but, in true Socratic fashion, to set up a yes-or-no moral judgment that he can proceed to annihilate in a most un-Socratic fashion, by his very exteriorness in relation to it:

> *Sganarelle:* . . . je n'approuve point votre méthode . . . je trouve fort vilain d'aimer de tous côtés comme vous faites. . . .
> *Dom Juan:* Il n'est rien qui puisse arrêter l'impétuosité de mes désirs [I. ii]

Dom Juan's semiotic behavior is virtually steeped in irony, and it is this mode which, when he does not remain silent and immobile, allows him to absent himself until such a time as he is sure of victory. For this reason, his conduct is best discussed in terms of nihilism rather than of negation; it would be a mistake to view his first long monologue either as a direct refutation of Sganarelle's proposition, "[Il est] fort vilain d'aimer de tous côtés," or as simply an expository address to the audience. While he does refer to Sganarelle in one sense, by ironizing his language (and, to a lesser extent, that of all the other characters), he does so only briefly, rapidly moving on to a discourse as foreign to the contemporary definition of context and meaning as he himself is. He reveals something of himself insofar as he takes a stand, but a stand so mobile that it rather suggests the modern notion of personal identity as a state of coherent change.

His opening line, permeated with images of monkish immobility that are made equivalent to tragic mutilation, which in turn equals death, ironizes a semiological style of life based on affirmation: "Quoi? tu veux qu'on se lie à demeurer au premier objet qui nous prend, qu'on renonce au monde pour lui et qu'on n'ait plus d'yeux pour personne?" (I. ii). Using Sganarelle's own word "demeurer" to modify the reflexive "se lier," Dom Juan detours its meaning toward a kind of suicidal crippling of the self in passive acquiescence to an object-aggressor ("qui nous prend"), thus endowing it with a cowardly, unmanly quality.[9] He functions in the world, in nature, where movement, activity, and aggression constitute the rules of the game, and women, like all the objects he encounters there, represent one more hostile force to be overcome by his will.

It may be helpful to us, and ineluctable for the other characters in the play, to speak in terms of an opposition between this "natural" world of perpetual and seemingly arbitrary change and a given culture presupposing an orderly, if infinite, succession of names that both designates and creates (represents) the world, but we must be careful to understand that Dom Juan's conduct in no way illustrates that opposition. His "nature" (both *who* and *where* he is) cannot be identified by dual structures because of the very irony of his ironic mode. As he moves on, he also erases, so that the "book" to which Sganarelle compares his speech either does not exist or is contained in his every separate, isolated word, gesture, sign, act, article of clothing, etc. Just as an ironic method of reading literary works — the stressing of the importance of an author's area of deliberate blindness, of the blindness of that commentary, and so on — may be either qualified as nihilistic or seen as an assurance of and metaphor for the continued flow of signs, so we find that Dom Juan and his conduct may mean either dangerous meaninglessness or perpetual possibilities of meaning. On the one hand, we assume the transcendence, and on the other, the immanence, of literary discourse.

Insofar as the play *Dom Juan* is concerned, there is a decided difficulty in that the main character moves on the circumference of a circle, neither inside nor outside it, but with a full view onto both sides of the tightrope he walks. He exploits the immanent quality of signs as though they simply solicited a reading, and proclaims his freedom to choose that reading, but remains fully aware of and prepared to profit from the other's automatically transcendent interpretation. When he says "marry me" to Elvire, he knows precisely what she will hear in his request, what anyone in his century would hear in it — its "rightful," Heaven-authorized meaning. He refuses to enter wholeheartedly, as it were, into the contract and commitment which he knows she assumes to be mutual on the grounds that, as he intimates to Sganarelle, he alone, not God or other men, determines his conduct. However, he must be careful not to let Elvire or any other object in the world know what he knows about his use of signs before he has triumphed over her. His freedom depends upon the deliberate destruction of her context, whence the symbolic value of her departure from the convent. The world for him is no primitive animal chaos out of which grow culture, men, order, and language, and from which these same differentiate themselves, but rather a present event whose coherence in relation to any other is marked only by the triumph of the will or the pursuit of pleasure. In order to move with and dominate that world of events, he must know and use, but remain detached from, contexts and definitions, lest he become "ridiculous," as he says of the faithful, like a book one enjoys and discards as he does all the objects his desire encounters.

Having interpreted Sganarelle's suggestion as a renunciation of the world, and therefore of the relationship between word-acts and that world, Dom Juan speaks of a tragic self-mutilation ("n'ait plus d'yeux pour personne?") that would seem both out of place in a comic work and patently foolish in a natural environment where self-affirmation depends upon the astute invocation of one's every physical resource. The subsequent death imagery, first implied and then stated ("s'ensevelir pour toujours dans une passion," "être mort dès sa jeunesse"), logically completes

77

his reduction to the absurdity of a cultural norm and prepares the way for a change in his use of irony. What follows seems to be a statement of policy, yet on closer examination we find a relentless use of transitive verbs which underline an apparent action / passion duality. His option for the former is coupled with such a powerful ironizing of conventional vocabulary and scrambling of meaning that the signification of that duality becomes dubious except perhaps when read ironically: ". . . toutes les belles ont droit de nous charmer, et l'avantage d'être rencontrée la première ne doit point dérober aux autres les justes prétentions qu'elles ont sur nos cœurs" (I. ii).

Dom Juan implies that by the very fact of their existence, beautiful women are the aggressors ("nous charmer," "les justes prétentions qu'elles ont sur nos cœurs"). At the same time, their potential for action depends upon his presence, for he encounters them, and not the contrary, before they engage him ("d'*être rencontrée . . .*"). What is more, since Sganarelle has invoked a principle of right and wrong, Dom Juan also speaks of the "right" to charm him and "just" claims. Tearing those words from their conventional moral context, however, he leaves us no frame of reference in which to interpret their meaning except the will to conquer that he affirms at the end of his monologue. If a claim *is just* because he *desires victory*, then his will, manifested by his stream of transitive verbs, constitutes the context of his (ironic) language. His implied judgment, the attribution of justice to a claim, or the rightfulness of seduction, undermines not only conventional moral values but the accepted theory and practice of verbal representation by ontological affirmation. Its referent is not the ambiguous interrelationship between the world, ideas, and words (ideas of things and ideas of signs), but the action of his desire on an object, a momentary appropriation whose significance is immediately erased by another subsequent and temporary abstraction of something from its context.

Dom Juan continues to undermine the active / passive duality with such pseudo oppositions as:

> la beauté me ravit . . .
> où je la trouve . . .
>
> je cède facilement . . . la violence dont elle nous entraîne.
> être engagé . . . n'engage point mon âme . . . [I. ii]

all of which he places in the "context" of "justice" and "in-justice" ("à faire injustice aux autres"), a frame of reference he can only safeguard by keeping his eyes open and active: ". . . je conserve des yeux pour voir le mérite de toutes, et rends à chacune les hommages et les tributs où la nature nous oblige" (I. ii) In addition, his actions become a paradoxically passive submission to a more powerful will, that of a "nature" which desires that he desire all beautiful women because they desire that he desire them! Once again, prisoners of judgment, we are reduced to tendering the sort of commentary that can only state that either (1) everyone is passive in Dom Juan's world or (2) everyone is active or (3) there are no such categories as action and passion. He himself sees only change: ". . . tout le plaisir de l'amour est dans le changement" (I. ii) — only petty victories that also resemble capitulation ("combattre par des transports") and the possibility of more of the same.

The question of the stasis / mobility duality thus also arises. Is there any real change in Dom Juan's repeated transitions? While he moves on, his path can be traced more by the above-mentioned circumference of a circle than by a linear progression, in that he seems to differentiate very little between and among the objects of his desire, which remains constant. In everyone else's terms, he "progresses" (i.e., *regresses*) from the heights of his noble birth to the depths of ignominy and death, that is, if we forcibly inscribe his conduct in the logocentric context that defines the Statue and the other characters, whatever their social status. He himself facilitates that inscription, as we shall see, when he abandons irony for pretense, when he enters a world of dualities and places himself in the wrong. Up to that point, however, and as long as no one realizes what he is doing before they have been victimized, he can quite safely continue to borrow, ironize, and discard people and signs, abstracting all things from their context and rendering them relative to him alone. Whence our epigraph: for Dom Juan possession is not that of objects useful in the world, but the tearing away of things from their function in order to strip them of any sense except in relation to him. Together, they define a circular semiotic enclosure in which he alone is subject, where he reigns as the meaning of any individual object. When he abstracts Elvire from her function as a nun, and attempts to abstract the young lady who causes his shipwreck and Charlotte from theirs as fiancées, his goal is to make their existence relative to his, to become the subject of their being.

Their difference resides only in chronology, not in essence, for they all refer back to him. He is the logos of a private collection of signs, symbols, and indices, a pure subjectivity, which as such cannot be described as either static or mobile. He is an ultimate principle which he refuses to define for the sake of his appetite and personal safety. His conduct can best be described as the systematic annihilation of the bond between signs and the world in order to temporarily tie the former to himself, thus replacing the latter. The flaw that will eventually put a stop to that conduct resides in the world's obedience to the Logos as contrasted with his refusal of that relationship.

Since to Dom Juan all objects are equal, in that they are equal to his desire and therefore equally desirable, he can only be stopped either by the completion of the series (the conquest of all beautiful women) or the snuffing out of his appetite, by the closing of the circle he wishes to draw or the elimination of its center. With these end-points lacking, he will continue his paradoxical repetition of different samenesses. As James Doolittle suggests: "Dom Juan's intention with any woman is not to set her naked on a pedestal to be admired for the beauty of her form, but to take her to his bed so that he may master her as a lover. For him the only valid criterion of beauty is the functional excellence of the beautiful object."[10] His only interest is in functionalism, and his goal is to so redirect that usefulness that it can only be defined in relation to him. Once he has achieved that goal, the individuality critical to him just a moment ago — its "functional excellence" — becomes sameness, an identity with others whose function he has been able to determine. When he declares himself unavailable for discussion of Sganarelle's remonstrances in Act I, scene ii ("Paix!"), it is because he has already demonstrated their irrelevance and is concerned with transforming a "jeune fiancée" (she is never identified in any other way), in all her potential functional excellence, into an Elvire, whose current functional conformity bores him totally. In apparently changing the subject, he is in reality only reaffirming it, as he stated in his monologue: it is and can only be a question of his desire. And his desire can only be to force everyone and everything to define themselves — their "meaning" — in relation to that desire, whence his plans to disturb the intelligence between fiancé and fiancée, to break their bond.

In addition to adroit questioning and irony, Dom Juan employs yet another means of withdrawing to the periphery of language. When Elvire appears in scene iii, he is faced not with a participant in an enemy system, a participant whom he wishes to engage permanently in the process of subjection without definitively conquering him (Sganarelle), nor with one he wishes to force into his own private system (Mathurine, Charlotte), but with a woman whose individuality already defines itself in relation to that system. His work is done, and he has only to encourage her to talk long enough to demonstrate the change he has effected in her situation. His initial silence, his refusal to exchange any corporal or verbal signs with her, fails only because of her exceptional strength and ability to confront that refusal with her own will: "Me ferez-vous la grâce, Dom Juan, de vouloir bien me reconnaître? et puis-je au moins espérer que vous daigniez tourner le visage de ce côté?" (I. iii). But his apparent submission to the demand conveyed by her questions and his admission of temporary disadvantage (". . . je vous avoue que je suis surpris") disarm her by the lack of pleasure they deliberately betray. She subsequently reveals her continuing passion for him and hints at the judgment she must make concerning a man who would discard his wife as lightly as has Dom Juan: ". . . j'en rejetais la voix qui vous rendait criminel à mes yeux" (I. iii).

At the same time, she offers to make a deal with him, proposing an exchange or contract which she knows he will respect no more than he did their marriage. She offers to suspend judgment if he will lie about his departure: "Parlez, Dom Juan, je vous prie, et voyons de quel air vous saurez vous justifier!" (I. iii). Dom Juan, however, does not participate in the equal exchange of signs but ironizes or devalues them, and then uses them in their transubstantiated condition to maneuver his interlocutor. He tosses the ball to Sganarelle, as though replying with a suggestion that she play with someone interested in her game. Desperate for a match, she acquiesces to his silence and turns to Sganarelle, revealing more and more of her mental state as she does so. But Sganarelle, eager to bend to his master's will and hopelessly ignorant of the particulars of his present desire, proves an inept partner:

> *Dom Juan:* Allons, parle donc à Madame.
> *Sganarelle:* Que voulez-vous que je dise?

[Elvire replies for Dom Juan, for in reality she cares a great deal, and Dom Juan very little, about the specific signs to be exchanged.]

*Dom Juan:* Tu ne répondras pas? . . .
Veux-tu répondre, te dis-je? [I. iii]

So Elvire again appeals to Dom Juan to emerge from his silence, but only on condition that he enter into the specific bargain she has proposed. When he consents to remain present — that is, to converse with her about his departure — he begins by mentioning the truth, once again evading her terms. She is then forced to interrupt with an attempt to humiliate him in an open statement of the contract she was trying to negotiate: "Ah! que vous savez mal vous défendre pour un homme de cour . . . J'ai pitié de vous voir la confusion que vous avez. Que ne vous armez-vous le front d'une noble effronterie?" (I. iii).

Elvire's strange invitation to play-acting in fact refers to an unrespected contract of the past, to their marriage, despite her use of the present tense. She recognized her defeat at Dom Juan's first glance, as soon as she arrived on stage, and yet, like him, she cannot easily renounce what she strongly desires, especially when she has been reduced to that desire, torn away from the context and meaning that defined her life before she met him. Like him, she wishes to draw her adversary into her own semiotic system, to force him to define himself in terms of her desire, but his silence and subsequent refusal to participate in a regulated exchange have robbed her of the arms she needs to accomplish her enterprise. Her only recourse is to a transcendent discourse, to a system of signs whose center is not her own desire but Heaven's will itself, whence the necessity of re-establishing her submission to that Principle. There is no irony or bad faith in her statement that she now fully knows Dom Juan, for she alone understands in depth why his use of signs and his conduct in general are invulnerable except to God.

It is Dom Juan's ironizing of the hypocritical attitude she has demanded of him that enlightens Elvire and moves her to affirm that she finally knows who he is. When the other characters — Gusman, Sganarelle, Pierrot, and Dom Louis — find that Dom Juan is not a truthful, honorable, law-abiding citizen of their community, they assume him to be a lying, cheating, rebellious criminal. In stating to Elvire that ". . . je n'ai point le

82

talent de dissimuler et . . . je porte un cœur sincère," and then proposing a blasphemous lie in a manner certain to prove his point (". . . j'ai ouvert les yeux de l'âme . . . Le repentir m'a pris, et j'ai craint le courroux céleste"), Dom Juan, who wants nothing more from Elvire, clearly establishes an absolute desire to remain outside the ideological and linguistic structure to which she adheres. When he refuses something, she therefore has no reason to believe that he will accept the opposite. He does not negate, for, as we saw in the case of Arnolphe's "Marriage Maxims," negation assumes the possibility of affirmation. Rather, Dom Juan annihilates; in his own system there is no binary organization of representation, no ambiguous floating referent nor a hierarchy of yes-or-no options. *He* is the universal referent, untroubled by any conflict between human and divine desire, or between human will and human understanding. (Since no one realizes how he functions until it is too late, his knowledge is always adequate to his will.) While the structure of conventional seventeenth-century signs might be represented by the following schema:

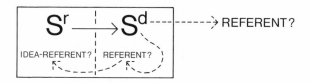

N.B. All linguistic terms and symbols or abbreviations thereof are taken directly from Saussure's *Cours de linguistique générale*.
$S^r$ = signifier ("signifiant")
$S^d$ = signified ("signifié")

with each sign related to others by an affirmative or negative form of the verb "to be," Dom Juan's discourse must be represented *in toto*:

83

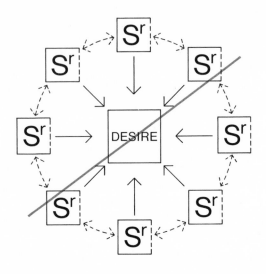

broken lines = conventional bonds severed by Dom Juan

solid lines = Dom Juan's purely temporary bonds

diagonal slash = cancellation's trace or simply *another way of representing the diagram itself*

Once the bond with the traditional signified is dissolved by an on-going process of irony, Dom Juan turns meaning toward himself, thus constructing an unmediated system. While his initial wish to destroy a tie may be mediated, as his desire for the unnamed female prey in Act I was originally kindled by the presence of her fiancé, his goal is to eliminate mediation between himself and the coveted object, and he does so with action, an elopement, a kidnapping, and a transitive verb. The above sketch portrays not the representation of representativeness — that is, mediation between things and words that fades out at the level of divine discourse — but a representation of desire that dissolves at the moment of enunciation, whence Dom Juan's "insaisissable" quality and the necessity of canceling the diagram as soon as it is drawn.

If God, a Logos, or any universal Principle other than his personal desire can be proven to exist, Dom Juan's system of non-signs will collapse. He would be removed from the center and obliged to act as a medium between things and words, or between that Principle and words, according to one's ideas about a referent in seventeenth-century grammar and logic.

When Elvire reappears in Act IV, scene vi, her understanding of the complexities of this situation has grown complete enough for her to realize that she must pose as a representative of that other desire, and not as her own. Yet she is once more defeated by Dom Juan's withdrawal, by his silence, and forced to retreat hastily ("Laissez-moi vite aller, ne faites aucune instance pour me conduire") lest she once again follow him to his periphery. The problem is precisely that she is posing — at least partially — and cannot retain the posture intended to indicate her recently recovered identity for any extended period of time without the reinforcement of Dom Juan's credulousness. As though fully reintegrated into her original linguistic and ideological context, she affirms that: "Ce n'*est* plus cette Done Elvire qui faisait des vœux contre vous" (IV. vi; my italics), offering a judgment about her faith and identity which either is or is not true but, in any case, is not up to her to make. Dom Juan's silence, once again, does not negate her negation but leaves her to flounder between the only two alternatives allowed in the system to which she has redeclared her allegiance. If she wishes to deal with him, she must use his own arms; since he has absented himself, since he will not be engaged in her battle for conversion, she would have to act accordingly in order to avoid the pitfalls of her recurring attraction to him. Instead, she bets on the strength of her role as divine spokeswoman, and hoping to reconquer and then define his presense, plunges herself into a situation in which she cannot win. If she has truly been reconverted, then according to the rules of her own linguistic system, her negation carries its opposite within it and dispenses Dom Juan, who realizes that Elvire is at a point of oscillation, from saying anything. She cannot leave that system unless she becomes someone else, in which case she would be abandoning it anyway. If, on the other hand, she has not been reconverted, then she still defines herself in terms of her desire for Dom Juan, still functions purely in relation to him, as one of a constellation of once-desired objects. When she begins her third speech ("Je vous ai aimé avec une tendresse extrême . . ."), we realize that the latter is the case.

Reversing her confusion of Act I, she uses a past tense to speak about a present emotion rushing forward to fill the void left by the silent Dom Juan.

In Act II, scene iv, we witness a further attempt on Dom Juan's part to reorganize people and signs around himself, but this time in the presence of two women he has not yet conquered. The acrobatic ballet executed between them, which terminates with a "Dom Juan, embarrassé,"[11] enacts the comic drama of an impending danger to his use of signs. Unless he is very careful and clever, the peasant women may escape Elvire's fate by discovering his strategy, and therefore his identity, as Elvire herself has pointed out, in time to disarm him. According to Jacques Guicharnaud's analysis of the play: "Si le couple Charlotte-Pierrot pouvait être considéré comme un parallèle libre et farcesque du couple Dom Juan-Elvire, l'intervention de Mathurine auprès de Dom Juan reprend la fonction d'Elvire auprès de Dom Juan, réduite au désir tout simple de la possession."[12] While each of the peasant girls' individual relationships to Dom Juan appears to conform to the latter's wishes, and Mathurine's untimely arrival to Elvire's discovery of his willful infidelity, the difference between this scene and scene iii, Act I, lies in the women's ability to communicate with each other as individuals. Their relationship predates Dom Juan's seduction attempts and is likely to survive them, a fact which impedes his present progress with each and partially explains his embarrassment when he must address them both at once. The sexual balance of the triangle is very much to his taste, but its internal dynamics are not. He cannot draw either of the women into the constellation represented in the above circular diagram as long as their desire for him is mediated by the other's presence. When Mathurine arrives, she immediately defines herself not only as Dom Juan's fiancée but also as Charlotte's rival. Her desire is single but double-edged, for she wishes both to conquer Dom Juan and to defeat Charlotte. Charlotte is in an identical situation, so that this disruption of Dom Juan's habitual pattern might be represented as follows:

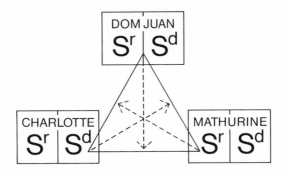

Solid lines = present situation
Broken lines = desired goals

Dom Juan finds himself no longer at the center of a circle, or even comfortably lodged between two women, but at one of three equidistant points on a triangle, *all three sides of which are stable*. The broken lines represent each person's aspiration to the center, the way each would like to destroy the triangular structure by converting it to a straight line, the extremities of which would constitute directly opposite points on the circumference of a circle, or its diameter, for Dom Juan (cf. above, p. 84 the "$S^r$" or half-signs). Everyone wishes to lop off the "signified" quality in the others' identities as signs and the "signifier" in him or herself. Mathurine and Charlotte maneuver with an eye to reducing Dom Juan to his desire for them, to defining him as a pure subject that would "mean" only in relation to who they are e.g.: "Dom Juan is my man"). If either could accomplish that, she would become a pure "signified," a referent or definitive principle in relation to the other two in this paradoxical system of nonmeaning, where each person acts like, and considers himself or herself to be, a pure active subject in order to become the single object of the other's desire and thus satisfy his or her own.

This particular situation can be designated as polygamous, in ideological terms, or "polysemic" in linguistic ones, in that all three people wish to wed the others to them in some sense. Dom Juan seeks temporary sexual possession capable of reaffirming his view and his use of signs in conjunction with desire. While the women function in a manner suggestive of Dom Juan's semiotic system in this scene, they are ultimately in search of definition. They each wish to permanently establish the following dual judgment by drawing it from his mouth:

| Dom Juan is my man. |
| --- |
| Charlotte (Mathurine) is my defeated rival. |

In order to break free of this contest of equal wills, a contest in which he has been appointed judge when he wishes to participate and win without letting Charlotte and Mathurine know he is doing so, Dom Juan must lie; he must offer a refutation of Charlotte's claim to Mathurine and vice versa. The fundamental "temporary / permanent" or "action / state of being" misunderstanding from which he has always profited with women and men alike must be maintained at all costs, even at the price of explicit pretense, of entry into everyone else's system of representation and judgment:

> *Mathurine* [à Dom Juan]: Monsieur, que faites-vous donc là avec Charlotte? Est-ce que vous lui parlez d'amour aussi?
> *Dom Juan:* Non, au contraire, c'est elle qui me témoignait une envie d'être ma femme, et je lui répondais que j'étais engagé à vous. [II. iv]

Dom Juan no longer ironizes, he reverses, momentarily consenting to a system of binary opposition ("au contraire") as he does so. By lying, he has accepted and chosen between two mutually exclusive alternatives, but having made the same choice with each of the women, he has also closed off the option of speaking to them collectively. Since he has said "yes and no" to their combined request for a "yes-or-no" judgment, and they are determined to clarify things ("Dites," "Parlez"), his only recourse is to retreat as quickly as possible to his familiar periphery. However, the path seems blocked behind him: prevarication has rendered futile any attempt at irony at this point, and the women will not permit him to be silent. Glancing desperately around him, he finally locates the wings and recognizes in them their potentially safe marginality and, in the very determination to act, a path to that safety:

88

> . . . il faut faire et non pas dire, et les effets décident
> mieux que les paroles. . . . l'on verra, quand je me
> marierai, laquelle des deux a mon cœur. . . .
>
> J'ai un petit ordre à donner; je viens vous retrouver dans
> un quart d'heure. [II. iv]

He has just barely re-established himself as a man of action,
for he is still juggling his preference for movement with emer-
gency concessions to a system which endows actions with the
power of definition. He forecasts an act that will announce the
person in relation to whom he defines himself as husband and
lover, regaining an equally precarious grip on irony. (Since he
probably intends either to marry both of them or neither of
them, a "decision" will indeed become clear, as well as the person
who occupies the center of his universe.) Nevertheless, his balance between two systems has been badly shaken at the end of
the scene, and he exits clumsily, to say the very least. This is the
first in a series of moments when he has to hide behind someone
else's sign (desire, clothes, attitude) instead of simply slipping
safely away to a periphery, as is his habit. With Charlotte and
Mathurine having momentarily cornered him, he could not easily
absent himself either verbally or bodily; Elvire's brothers and
Dom Louis will, in turn, do the same, thus preparing the Statue's
final victory.

Thanks to Sganarelle's efforts to enlighten Charlotte and
Mathurine, Dom Juan can return to the stage feeling somewhat
less pressured, regain his composure by silently pressuring Sganarelle ("Oui," "Sganarelle," "Hon!"), and then, thanks to a new
crisis, re-exit, with his manly self-image intact. Yet even as his
tone with the two women recaptures a self-assured, authoritative
quality at the end of the scene, he plunges further into a contradiction between the two mutually exclusive but interdependent
terms of a duality. In his opening monologue he had set up a differentiation between his behavior and the existence Sganarelle
advocated, without allowing that differentiation to fall into a
coupling of opposites. Constantly invoking irony, he simply dis-
tanced himself more and more from his interlocutor, until he
could ignore him completely and speak only in terms of his own
active desire. When he hears that twelve mounted men are in
pursuit of him, he again determines to act, but in a manner he
himself deemed unmanly when challenged by Elvire.

In his usual fashion, he decides to retreat, to slip out from under the pressure exerted, but instead of doing so by erasing the path that lies behind him, he takes cover in the world of definable personal identity, that very world into which no one had previously been able to lure him. He adopts a disguise, implying a stable, recognizable persona that must be hidden. Subscribing to a lie, he also admits the possibility of truth, and attempts to do so under a secondary disguise, that of his previous semiotic conduct: "Comme la partie n'est pas égale, il faut user de stratagème, et éluder adroitement le malheur qui me cherche. Je veux que Sganarelle se revête de mes habits" (II. v). His first sentence sounds like a description of his behavior with Sganarelle and Elvire. He is always outnumbered (for even when he is talking with one person, the other always carries with him the authority of a whole "semiologos" or linguistic community), and, adroitly elusive, he manages to wield irony cleverly enough to escape to a realm beyond their jurisdiction. His second sentence therefore comes as something of a surprise. Can it be that that whole process has suddenly been defined as taking cover behind a lie? Has he then abandoned rapid, agile movement for comfortable immobility? It would seem so, in light of his very recent antics with Charlotte and Mathurine. Events have suddenly accelerated to a pace he apparently feels he cannot surpass, so he hides behind someone else's system of signs. Under the force of numbers, his faith in his ability to elude seems to collapse, for he never considers the possibility of out-maneuvering his pursuers, either physically or verbally. To add insult to injury, he *defines* that conduct with a further prevarication, assimilating it to behavior whose very "insaisissable" quality he had fondly nourished when able to move faster and more diversely than his past words and deeds.

Sganarelle, who has been preoccupied with a feeling of impending danger and even death from his very first attempt to sway Dom Juan (I. ii), fully realizes the implications of his master's decision, albeit in his usual farcical manner:

> Monsieur, vous vous moquez. M'exposer à être tué sous vos habits, et . . .

> O Ciel, puisqu'il s'agit de mort, fais-moi la grâce de n'être point pris pour un autre! (II. v)

Throughout the play he has been caught between two linguistic and ideological systems, Dom Juan's and the one everybody else, including Heaven itself, espouses. As a result, and with considerably less agility, he must continually execute a ballet not unlike Dom Juan's performance with Mathurine and Charlotte. If he affirms himself in opposition to his master in order to exonerate himself vis-à-vis divine judgment, he runs the risk of physical punishment. If he fails to do so, he may have to share the horrible fate that is certain to befall Dom Juan. He therefore continually bends to the latter's will and serves an evil cause, but, his admiration for and frequent attempts to imitate his master notwithstanding, he protests as frequently as seems prudent. Each time Dom Juan appears unexpectedly, as with Gusman and the peasant girls, or adopts a threatening tone, he demonstrates with an abrupt about-face that he considers himself to be acting under duress. However, he also tries to undo his own contribution to his master's success whenever he finds himself alone with a victim, which would imply a haunting feeling of responsibility for his actions. Since he wishes to assure his present physical safety and comfort in Dom Juan's continued service, as well as his future spiritual well-being, he must often juggle his words and actions, translating them from one feared authority's rules of exchange into the other's, according to who happens to be listening. His inevitable clumsiness, contrasted with the necessity of lightning speed, sometimes produces a senseless mid-system scramble, as when he learns of his master's hypocrisy and cannot dissociate himself from it quickly enough (V. ii).

Sganarelle does in fact possess considerably less talent for acting and a weaker grasp of semiotic behavior than his situation seems to demand, yet it is his very ignorance and gracelessness that permit him to continue functioning in it. Dom Juan's mode of signifying depends upon absolute solitude as the perpetrator of that mode, a condition which Sganarelle helps to fulfill without perceiving the adequacy of his inadequate responses. The master does not desire any profound loyalty from his servant in the sense of an allegiance to his conduct, but rather just what he always obtains — submission in spite of self. The transparency of Sganarelle's performance merely constitutes pleasant proof of the requisite ersatz submission. Their relationship, unlike any other of Dom Juan's, remains permanent, and that permanence calls for a unique brand of obedience without any modification of identity. In reality, Sganarelle need expend much less energy on pleasing his master than he does, since the order calls for feigned agreement, not heartfelt approval. Sganarelle knows how Dom Juan acts. If he were to submit as did Elvire (or to truly convince Dom Juan of his submission), redefining himself entirely in relation to Dom Juan's desire, he would become a competitor for the center of the circle, for the point of reference, just as Elvire was in Act I and will again be, as God's representative, in Act IV, and just as Charlotte and Mathurine threatened to become. In general, if Dom Juan has won when another begins to fight, he finds the competition uninteresting and slips away from his victim. If he has not, he tries to stop it by lying about what he is doing, as with the peasant girls. Since Sganarelle knows from the outset what happens to those who give themselves over, and since Dom Juan does not wish to sever their tie, the latter requires his servant to do his bidding yet remain faithful to himself, thus precluding any sort of definitive conquest.

When Dom Juan decides to confiscate his valet's costume and thus act the role of the bad actor, Sganarelle realizes that the usual dynamics of their relationship, of which he was never fully aware, have changed. He has now been ordered to produce a convincing performance, costume and all, in order that the spectators accept the signs he displays and the indices he communicates as significative of his identity. Suddenly Dom Juan requires a (false) context and in order to secure it, orders his valet to persuade everyone that it is he, Sganarelle, who wishes to build the mobile system whose access had been forbidden him. The better the show, the more likely he is to succumb to the applause and — since Sganarelle's heaven resembles just one more spectator — to suffer eternal damnation for his sinfully successful performance. His only hope is to convince Dom Juan that there is room for them both in the world of truth and lie. By the beginning of Act III he has already succeeded and wastes no time at proving himself their own most gullible spectator.[13]

Act III takes place in a forest, a context which again raises the ambiguous question of a possible "nature / culture" duality, especially in relation to Act IV, in which events are entirely confined to Dom Juan's apartment, that is, a culturally defined, enclosed space. As I discussed above, while an experience of "nature" is central to and forms a backdrop for Dom Juan's autonomy in the exchange of signs, he generally eludes any behavior which would define that concept in opposition to "culture." His recourse to lies, and his thus inverted reweaving of conventional ties between signs and the world, have already problematized the survival of the Domjuanesque idea of the natural world; his encounter with the Poor Man in Act III, scene ii, virtually annihilates it in the same way as he himself had habitually swept away the significance of his own gestures. This time, however, it is the other who acts upon him. The reason for invoking a metaphor of the bottom of a descending spiral for this encounter thus becomes clear. Dom Juan's dialogue with the Poor Man both highlights the autonomous nature of his enterprise and demonstrates its impossibility in the presence of a man who has chosen his semiotic behavior in an even more autonomous manner. The dual menace of the Poor Man's refusal to be seduced and the other characters' growing awareness of Dom Juan's strategy mark the onset of an evaporation of the latter's free will and prepare his full-scale retreat into a Tartuffe-like role.

"The ignominy of his fellow characters lies not in their fidelity to the conventions, but in the extent to which, bending their wills to confine, deform, and vitiate their dignity as individual men, they voluntarily enslave themselves to authorities of their own making."[14] Thus James Doolittle explicates Dom Juan's exceptional respect for the Poor Man's "humanity" and his subsequent willingness to give him a gold piece as a nonironic sign of straightforward admiration, the recognition of a virile brother whom he can neither conquer nor elude. According to Doolittle, then, Dom Juan permits stabilization in the meaning of his communications when he speaks with someone unwilling to "vitiate his dignity" in order to participate in a linguistic community or obtain physical comfort, regardless of his interlocutor's ideology. If we delve into this "met-his-match" explanation of Dom Juan's final gift, keeping our own interest in Molière's characters' behavior in mind, we find a contest between a man who has had to defy Ultimate Authority in order to freely redefine patterns of exchange as separate empirical events and another who is able to submit and serve that Authority without any deformation of his will or identity. The Poor Man actually appears freer of a yes-or-no language of judgment, to which he nevertheless acquiesces, than Dom Juan, who must live in continual bad faith, hiding the fact of his defiance by way of substitution. The latter has only been able to avoid purely ontological statements by replacing them with verbs of action whose meaning relative to preceding and subsequent enunciations remains unclear. He has had to annihilate both mediation and context rapidly enough to evade angry victims, while the Poor Man can function freely within the conventional linguistic system by requesting others to satisfy his appetite, rather than maneuvering them into it, all the while stubbornly adhering to a self-determined personal identity. This beggar, who dwells as much in the ill-defined expanse of an ambiguous nature as does Dom Juan himself,[15] has secured a freedom and individual integrity that threaten no one, not even the Don, who, failing to realize the importance of the Poor Man's response, experiences this incident as lightly as his near drowning while trying to kidnap the "jeune fiancée" of Act I.

Were he to take note of the reply he receives, he might glimpse the fundamental flaw in his "autonomous" use of signs. Upon hearing the beggar's kindly warning about thieves in the forest and his subsequent request for alms, Dom Juan mistakenly places him in the category of contemptible men and women, of whom Sganarelle is an extreme yet archetypal example: "Ah! ah! ton avis est intéressé, à ce que je vois" (III. ii). He sees a man driving a bargain and, as usual, seeks to avoid his assigned role in the negotiations: ". . . prie-le qu'il te donne un habit, sans te mettre en peine des affaires des autres" (III. ii). Since the terms of the bargain are explicit enough to be unavoidable (Dom Juan must either give the gold piece or not), he cannot appear to agree and then withdraw to an uncommitted periphery, as with Elvire. Assuming the beggar's vile submission and the twisting of his will under an authority created for that purpose, Dom Juan proposes an alternative bargain which would reduce the Poor Man to Sganarelle's status: Heaven is his master; then Heaven must fill his needs. If, on the other hand, Dom Juan fills the Poor Man's needs, then the latter must abjure Heaven and accept him as master: "Tu n'as qu'à voir si tu veux gagner un louis d'or ou non. En voici un que je te donne, si tu jures; tiens, il faut jurer" (III. ii).

In establishing and mocking the beggar's dire necessity, Dom Juan has simply and mistakenly presumed the former's submission to an inadequate master whom he can easily replace. The bargain, however, is not between the beggar and God, for his faith remains unconditional, but with other men, *none* of whom he will accept as master. His refusal to submit inevitably draws Dom Juan into a logocentric yet nonhierarchical linguistic universe: the Poor Man treats his words as subject to Divine Truth, and his person as equal to his own in human dignity. Dom Juan

94

salutes this truly viable alternative to Heaven-authorized societal convention, the elimination of the middle term, with a gold piece, accepting the Poor Man as his equal. Yet since he does not in fact see all people as equals, cannot check his will to dominate others, and considers faith in God an unnecessary infringement upon his autonomous use of signs, their paths have crossed only momentarily. They will subsequently continue their divergent courses, for Dom Juan cannot afford to comprehend the immediate critical relevance of that crossroads to his own separate course in the play.

The precipitation of events continues to deluge Dom Juan, but even though he is tracked, his encounter with Elvire's brothers constitutes a kind of breathing space for him. Both Carlos and Alonse have willingly subjected themselves to externally imposed, often conflicting social sanctions, and their behavior according to principle (gratitude, honor, vengeance, etc.) allows Dom Juan to behave as he did at the beginning of the play. In Act III, scene iii, when he comes to Dom Carlos's aid, he hides his identity by ironizing it:

> Il est un peu de mes amis, et ce serait à moi une espèce de lâcheté, que d'en ouir du mal. . . .

> Je suis si attaché à Dom Juan qu'il ne saurait se battre que je ne me batte aussi [III. iii]

Thus he accepts the challenge, but removes it to a time and place either more favorable to victory or perhaps nonexistent, while Carlos acquiesces to his every condition out of gratitude to a man who has saved his life (in marked contrast to Dom Juan's treatment of Pierrot). When Alonse appears, recognizes him, and moves in for the kill, Dom Juan has only to step back and wait for the brothers' conflicting and equally absolute priorities to defeat each other and free him. For the first time in the play, he "identifies" himself: "Oui, je suis Dom Juan moi-même, et l'avantage du nombre ne m'obligera pas à vouloir déguiser mon nom" (III. iii), but in such a tautological manner ("je . . . moi-même") that he totally eludes the usual explicative or descriptive function of names assigned to things, and thus, in spite of an apparent affirmation, avoids any judgment about himself in the Port-Royal sense. Coupled with the gesture which accompanies it ("mettant fièrement la main sur la garde de son épée"), his statement becomes an aggressive act fully consistent with his notion of manly valor. In telling Dom Carlos who he is, he responds physically to a physical challenge from other men for the same reasons that he rushed to Carlos's aid in the first place. As he freezes in the pose assumed when he affirmed his readiness to defend himself, his statement must be read more as an analogue for physical courage than as a verbal revelation about himself.

In the same way, Dom Juan's response to Carlos's plight and the stage directions which follow:

> Mais que vois-je là? un homme attaqué par trois autres? La partie est trop inégale, et je ne dois pas souffrir cette lâcheté.
>
> (Il court au lieu du combat.) [III. ii]

belonged to a single pattern of exchange. In both cases he remains faithful to his continual *reductio ad absurdum* of the isolation of semiotic behavior into rigorously controlled separate systems. His words and his actions refer only to himself; his physical and verbal gestures must be read as strictly interchangeable equivalents whose meaning remains as ambiguous as any of his behavior. His subsequent immobility refers in turn to an option for silent withdrawal, the return to a safe periphery. When Carlos once again addresses him, he replies from his marginal habitat that, for his part, he has struck no bargain, that he owes Carlos no gratitude, but will appear and defend himself as originally promised: "Je n'ai rien exigé de vous, et vous tiendrai ce que j'ai promis" (III. iv).

Dom Juan's first encounter with the Statue is of an altogether different nature. The Statue does not serve priorities, it establishes them, and elects other characters to speak for them (Sganarelle, Elvire, Dom Louis). Dom Juan can thus rise to the challenge of its presence by inviting it to dinner just as he had once challenged the Commander and has recently challenged Dom Carlos to a duel. However, he cannot seem to elude its silence as he could the two brothers' verbosity. As a representation of the Commander, it merits the mockery Dom Juan heaps on it: "Parbleu! le voilà bon, avec son habit d'empereur romain!" (III. v). His comment portrays the Commander as a very silly man indeed, one who wasted a lifetime of potential pleasure for a magnificently petrified gesture, a permanent stasis so grandiose that it becomes patently ridiculous: ". . . on ne peut voir aller plus loin l'ambition d'un homme mort; et ce que je trouve admirable, c'est qu'un homme qui s'est passé, durant sa vie, d'une assez simple demeure, en veuille avoir une si magnifique pour quand il n'en a plus que faire" (III. v). The tomb and statue are absurd to him because they serve no present purpose vis-à-vis the Commander, and therefore have no function that Dom Juan may dislocate and turn toward himself. Yet the Commander's pretentious imitation of immortality represents a challenge. He is aware that its conventional Caesarean vainglory signifies the very opposite of the Commander's attitude toward self-indulgence and aggrandizement while he was alive; he therefore correctly perceives the edifice before him in the context of a logocentric system of signs based on mediation, and cannot resist the temptation to once again demonstrate his disdain for and immunity to that system.

Assuming that the Statue, like the Commander himself, represents one more servile medium. between Heaven and earth, a representation of that use of signs which rigorously respects societal convention and man-made heavenly decrees concerning the source-guarantee of Truth and Meaning, Dom Juan gleefully mocks its (and the Commander's) self-imposed enslavement to conventional patterns of exchange:

> *Sganarelle:* . . . je pense qu'il ne prend pas plaisir de nous voir.
> *Dom Juan:* Il aurait tort, et ce serait mal recevoir l'honneur que je lui fais. [III. v]

Were things as Dom Juan believes them to be, the subsequent invitation to dinner and the marble's dumbness would successfully highlight its contemptible self-deprivation of appetite and will. Sganarelle, seeking, as usual, to escape a danger in which his master has once more placed him, inadvertently makes a poignant observation about Dom Juan's impious playfulness: "Vous moquez-vous? Ce serait être fou que d'aller parler à une statue" (III. v). If it is true that Dom Juan feels only scorn for this spectacular semiotic absurdity, for the impossible representation of an eternalized unleashing of human will rendered meaningless by the represented's lifetime of submission, then why is he having such a good time *establishing* its absurdity? Elvire was a boring, importunate nuisance, presumably because she had given herself entirely to him. Yet the statue of a man whose life has perhaps been arbitrarily sacrificed to Dom Juan's will, for reasons left unstated, and more importantly, without any special or lasting significance for Dom Juan, distracts him.

His determination to prove Sganarelle's fears groundless seems unconvincing, since he has never been interested in his valet's ideas or reactions except as a means to his own ends, unless he has some personal investment in eliminating that terror. He surely does not believe that this hideous museum piece could represent a Divine Authority in whose existence or nonexistence he claims total disinterest — until and if he should have to deal with it. However, recent events have awakened in him a momentary concern about the viability of his habitual employ of people and signs. Since his attempts to seduce the young fiancée, Mathurine, Charlotte, and the Poor Man have all been thwarted and his personal safety endangered, the power of his will, in relation to the universal agreement to refer ultimate responsibility for signs and personal identity to a transcendent ideology, inevitably comes into question. Sganarelle's trembling as such does not interest Dom Juan, but as a laughable extreme, as the parody of unconditional allegiance to a language of alternative, transcendent, ontological judgments, his valet's reaction assumes universal significance. Unwilling to confront a group of events as a significant whole which indicates that his appetite has been denied and his autonomy compromised, Dom Juan suddenly feels a fleeting need to prove Sganarelle's cowardliness: "Viens, maraud, viens, je te veux bien faire toucher au doigt ta poltronnerie" (III. v). He continues to treat the present as a context-free act, an arbitrary ahistorical event, yet his furious determination to force Sganarelle to speak, and then to test this inert mass's ability to exchange signs, seem disproportionate to the situation, unless we read it in the context of the recent past. Similarly, it becomes a question of whether a monumentalized gesture fails to signify anything other than poor taste or refers to the very enforcement of semiotic conventions in which Dom Juan's contemporaries participate and to which they submit.

Once the Statue has accepted the invitation to dinner, participation in and submission to the community's decrees about the bond between signs and the world and its rigid regulation of semiotic exchange becomes the logical, necessary result of the existence of Divine Truth. If Dom Juan, in turn, accepts the failure of his experiment, sees and reads the Statue's reply, then he must also understand that human language either is or is not in harmony with truth, and that his behavior constitutes a whole, each act of which affirms his disharmony with a context which does in fact exist. His only recourse is to abandon the situation ("Allons, sortons d'ici"), as he did his predicament with Mathurine and Charlotte, in order to move rapidly on to another hopefully unrelated adventure, to in fact annihilate the event by denying it any meaning: ". . . nous pouvons avoir été trompés par un faux jour, ou surpris de quelque vapeur qui nous ait troublé la vue" (IV. i).

The very necessity of purposefully severing himself from Act III at the opening of Act IV ("laissons cela") indicates that Dom Juan can no longer evade the fact of interrelationships among words and acts. A context, his own, is now closing around him just as surely as the linear progression of speeches, scenes, and acts in the play refers each part to the others and to Dom Juan's eternal damnation — the end-point, meaning, or internal / external "referent" of the play.[16] The succession of intruders in Act IV, only one of whom, M. Dimanche, is foolish enough to accept Dom Juan's ironic gestures literally, and thereby lose his own and the Don's path entirely, merely illustrates the tightening of a circle around him. As in *L'Ecole des femmes*, the impossibility of the protagonist's rebellion against the natural order of things and words has been amply demonstrated by the end of Act III, and it remains only to trace the particulars of his downfall. And, again, it is the protagonist's refusal to perceive the abundant evidence of his defeat that keeps the plot moving and the other characters fighting with him until he can be silenced by some voice representative of Nature or Order.

As for Dom Juan, he cannot believe that a nature so unnatural, a rational order created by men who declare it to be an accord between human and divine will and thus the "natural" order, could possess the power to destroy his own personal endeavor, to arrest his movement. Men carved the Statue from stone, and whatever its mystery, submission to it can only constitute cowardice. Thus Dom Juan uses the word "repentir" in Act V, scene v, indicating an acceptance of the universal interpretation of his behavior as the defiance of a sacred power greater than he, but will not give in to a man-made statue pretending to represent that power. In Act IV he cannot eat his dinner because Dom Louis, Elvire, and the Statue, who have all at some point sworn allegiance to the True Center (or circumference, according to one's location of the Universal Referent) of the only legitimate semio-ideological system and have thereby deputized themselves in the effort to prevent any further indulgence of his appetite, all seek to bring Dom Juan to justice. Yet he persists in acting, on the one hand, as though each visit were unrelated to the others and as though the repeated deprivation of his appetite were an accidental, arbitrary event unrelated to his other failures, and, on the other hand, as though he needed to take cover from a cumulative barrage, whence his recourse to hypocrisy in Act V. Sganarelle's hysterical condemnation in Act V, scene ii, both highlights and satirizes the seriousness of the community's urgent need to destroy a man who will thus participate in a definition of his conduct as "evil," but will not cease, because he cannot admit having met anyone powerful enough to thwart him.

From "insaisissable," Dom Juan has become accessible, readily understandable to any reader of his century, and has thus finally wandered into the mysterious Statue's realm of jurisdiction. Suddenly, in Act V, nature, for Dom Juan also, becomes that order of things in which men remain eternally vulnerable to the Truth: his nudity has become as embarrassing as Arnolphe's animality and as necessary as the latter's association of nakedness, the inability to speak, and the failure to force others to do his bidding (*L'Ecole des femmes*, II. ii). Dom Juan can no more acknowledge his relationship to a Divine Speaker, to human flesh, or to bread or stone as the Word incarnate, than Arnolphe can acquiesce to the power of the natural order of culture, or Tartuffe to social control over the quality, distribution, and exchange of signs. He will succumb only to the combined vengeance of God and men, to that strangely immanent yet ultimately transcendent Meaning he sought to replace. In order for his past victims — that circle of once wholly dependent signifiers depicted in my diagrammatic representation of his discourse — to close around and suffocate his desire, reaffirming the wholeness of each individual's will, identity, and meaning, a mysterious Ultimate Irony must also annihilate his present discourse in the same way as he himself sought to erase the significance of his words and acts behind him. Sganarelle, like M. Dimanche, must go unsalaried because individual claims to the fair exchange of signs and currency are of very little importance unless, like Elvire's, Dom Louis's — and perhaps Molière's — they are made in the service of a *Sēmē* beyond the self.[17]

## 4

## Counterpoint:
## The *Trompe-L'Œil* Bas-Relief,
## or Misrepresentation Meaning Presence

> "Et suivant ce qu'on peut être,
> Les choses changent de nom."
>> *Amphitryon*, I. i. 130–31

> *Sosie:* Non, Monsieur, c'est la vérité pure.
> Ce moi plutôt que moi s'est au logis trouvé;
> Et j'étais venu, je vous jure,
> Avant que je ne fusse arrivé.
> *Amphitryon:* D'où peut procéder, je te prie,
> Ce galimatias maudit?
> Est-ce songe? Est-ce ivrognerie?
> Aliénation d'esprit?
> Ou méchante plaisanterie?
> *Sosie:* Non: c'est la chose comme elle est,
> Et point du tout conte frivole.
>> *Amphitryon*, II. i. 740–50

In the preceding three chapters, I have tried to isolate in Molière's texts ways in which his discourse represents the French classical notion of language as a particular case of representation and as the representativeness and representability of that capacity. In the process, it became apparent (1) that discourse not only is a means of representing the struggle to dominate the world and the other, but also constitutes that which the self — Arnolphe — sought to monopolize: power itself. It also became clear that (2) through certain prohibitions placed on the construction and exchange of signs — on the will to error, on the annihilation of the bond linking part to whole and the subsequent negation of the system's ultimate authorization by some "external" Logos — that discourse, as well as other semiotic systems, can constitute one way of representing the classical experience of order.[1] They there-

101

fore remain inseparable from laws of exchange, from desire, and from power. Implicit in Molière's plays is the affirmation that *there is order*; the representative worth of words and the laws of exchange constitute models of that order, whose function it is to organize and control both the means and the objects of desire.

In selecting *Amphitryon* for my final consideration, I wish to emphasize, both by comparison and contrast, an additional modality of those uses of signs and that experience of order. While it must be taken into account in a semiology of meaning designed to aid in interpreting *L'Ecole des femmes*, *Tartuffe*, and *Dom Juan*, that modality appears absolutely central to *Amphitryon:* the originality of personal identity and its relationship to truth.

In Chapters 2 and 3 I emphasized the separation (as well as the inseparability) of things and words inherent in classical culture and the accompanying rarefication of discourse in its mediate position between thought and experience — ideally, to the point of its eventual transparency. Clarity, according to the Port-Royal *Grammar* and *Logic*, is both assumed to be the natural property of pure signs, and because of human propensity for equivocation and rhetoric, constitutes the prescribed goal of any semiotic system. From a modern point of view, this attribution of the opaque materiality of discourse to unnecessary figures and tropes seems paradoxical in that it reflects both the primacy of discourse and its self-rarefication into an "immediate medium," or nonexistence, in favor of reality, being, or things, at least as they present themselves to the mind (i.e. "clear ideas"). Words would seem to occupy the very center of speculation about knowledge in a culture perpetually concerned with an omnipresent logos, with endless rational principles that together "say" the Reason or Truth of the world. Speech itself, which seems to be the central theme of the three plays already discussed, is very much a reality and of considerable import. Although in *Dom Juan* the (theo)Logos is represented by a mobile mass of stone that says very little, a thing whose imposing reality bypasses the need for words, the Statue's massive materiality and relative silence also reflect a kind of neutralization of discourse in its function as a medium between the subject "I" (both Molière and the audience or reader) and his experience of physical reality. The Statue possesses a secret meaning which, in its absence, the various characters' discourse had only to indicate, as though speech could be decoded rather than interpreted. When it appears and physically touches Dom Juan, it puts an end to idiolect, speech, and the play itself, since its "meaning" has become clear even to Dom Juan by the fact of its manifest reality, its massive presence. The question arises as to whether the stone represents the Word or whether it represents words representing stone. Paradoxically, the quintessential logos *is* the thing in itself or its own evanescence. In the passage quoted above, Sosie and Amphitryon struggle with a similar contradiction.

The separation of things and words in fact constitutes a necessary condition for the signifying of the former by the latter, and marks the primacy of the order of things as represented and representable in a systematic organization of verbal signs. The world demonstrates a rational order, which, in the absence of that world's original, material reality (in a text, on a stage), discourse has only to indicate. However, it must do so without developing its own "truth," without interposing a false reality or mask (as, for example, Tartuffe's elaborate rhetoric symbolizes and sometimes indexes his sham) whose opacity would garble our conception of things as they are. There is thus a considerable problem, since words both indicate ideas or representations and manifest themselves, and so remain continually suspect because of their power to obscure or distort our view of the world. The abundant attention given to discourse in the seventeenth century reflects a concern with preventing and curing the sign's opacity — with the purity of representation — more than it does an appreciation of language per se.

One way in which the desire to dematerialize signs manifests itself within discourse in the seventeenth century is indicated in the relatively new importance accorded to literary authorship, both insofar as entire works are concerned and within the texts themselves: the subject of a speech or text is also its founder and originator, and therefore retains the responsibility for its unity and coherence. The subject is expected to know and articulate the meaning concealed in his discourse. His biography, the "real" historical events surrounding the genesis of his speech or text, and any additional discourse attributable to him may all contribute to that articulation. It is as though his unique intuition grasped and translated the world's sense in various series of signs forming chains of representation, judgment, reason, and order.

Thus, in the passage from *Amphitryon* quoted above, Sosie speaks of a world order which he scrupulously respects — an order of the "pure truth" and "the thing as it is" — on exactly the same level, in fact equating the two. The "thing" in question is of course an event, his initial encounter with Mercury, the reality or existence of which he must establish by proving the truth of a second event, the story he is in the process of telling. His narrative must attain a sufficient degree of transparency for Amphitryon to "see" the "reality" of a happening external to discourse — the model, idea, or perception that Sosie wishes to represent. Amphitryon necessarily finds it difficult to believe him, since, according to the rules of current semiotic praxis, Sosie cannot possibly, like Jupiter, be himself and his opposite at the same time, both the subject and the object of event and narrative alike. Were that the case, he would prove capable of at once being, presenting, and representing — that is, of *creating* truth from nothingness.

Were he to write an autobiography, Sosie might represent himself, the writer, at another point in time, as an*other* self, but not that previous self and someone else; in the former case, difference would serve to delineate identity, to establish continuity and sameness. On the contrary, he attests to the originality of two identical opposite selves; he, the speaker, recounts a dialogue that took place at a single moment in time between Sosie the brave and Sosie the weak (II. 800–06), only one of whom bears any resemblance to him at present. It is no wonder that Amphitryon has difficulty in taking him seriously. In the context of a culture characterized by rationalism in science and the baroque in art, Amphitryon can only interpret Sosie's tale of resemblance as one of those frequent illusions of which Descartes warns,[2] either an enormous *quiproquo* or some kind of marginal discourse not to be understood in the same way as rational, factual speech.

As we saw with regard to the portraits in *Tartuffe*,[3] Molière's is an age of the deceptive senses, one in which resemblance constitutes a tempting pitfall in the search for certainty rather than acceptable evidence of sameness. Sosie can hardly expect to establish a fact by stating that Mercury *looks* like him: "Des pieds jusqu'à la tête, il est comme moi fait" (II. i. 783), particularly in view of the comic contrasts he mixes into his statement of similarity ("Beau, l'air noble," etc.), the whole of which constitutes the self-annihilating judgment that Mercury both is and is not Sosie and vice versa.

One may object that *Amphitryon* does not, like *Tartuffe*, exhibit any expressly didactic quality, and that it would thus be risky to read Sosie's attempts to establish the truth of his experiences with Mercùry as a parody of scientific method. This is, after all, a thoroughly baroque play in which Molière delights in toying with comic illusion, doubles, and *quiproquo* situations, all of which, by a twist of the supernatural, turn out to be illusory illusions or the "truth" of comedy. The urgent need for a demonstrable differentiation between appearances and reality gives way in *Amphitryon* to a playful hodgepodge of the two, which, by virtue of an intervention of that "merveilleux" recently exiled from the domain of rational discourse and relegated to poetry,[4] is redefined as "fact" by a Dom Juan not only excused but canonized, a divinity the arbitrariness of whose will is rivaled only by the impetuousness of his desire. Indeed, Molière seems in this play to have abandoned the tightrope he so often walked between morals and aesthetics in favor of a momentary but total indulgence in pure entertainment.

I would stress, however, that it is not Sosie's identity that has been called into question for Amphitryon — although his state of mind may have been — but rather the existence of his double, as well as that of someone so similar to Amphitryon himself that he could cause Alcmène to be unfaithful without casting the merest shadow of a doubt on her intention and desire to remain loyal to her spouse. Similarity here is not only an entertaining game of the mind and senses, a pleasurable occasion for the confusion of two differences, it also provides an opportunity for the generally impossible differentiation of sameness. As Charles Mauron points out in his discussion of Bergson's thesis concerning the comedy of imitation: ". . . il faut bien noter que le rire provient d'une différence entre le changement attendu et la répétition en tant que telle."[5] Comedy is thus double and doubles back on itself in the passage from Molière which opens this chapter, for it is not only the difference between Amphitryon's expectations and Sosie's story of repetition that provokes laughter. Sosie also repeats repetition, which, like the proverbial cracked phonograph record, rapidly ceases to amuse Amphitryon, to the point that his increasing frustration and ire provide a new source of comedy.

Resemblance no longer resembles itself in this work — that is, it is no longer an illusion as Amphitryon believes it to be until Act III, scene x, and as indeed it *should* be in a typically baroque plot. This play in fact re-rationalizes the baroque by out-baroquing it in a sense.[6] Real illusions (Sosie's and Amphitryon's doubles) cause an illusory reality (Alcmène's infidelity), which in turn reveals itself as superhuman fact or verifiable identity! For Amphitryon it is as though a "trompe-l'œil" turned out to be a three-dimensional Statue, converted by Dom Juan and rendered exceedingly mobile — *sic transit gloria numinis*. Alcmène can be successfully seduced by an Olympian, but only one clever and powerful enough to reproduce Amphitryon's every quality and gesture. Thus in order to satisfy their divine desires, the gods are reduced to participation in a system of signs designed and controlled by men, constrained to that metamorphosis of the will to which Dom Juan remained largely immune until annihilated by his own willful conversion to participation.

Of course, the difference lies in Jupiter's divine prerogative: he need not struggle to remain peripheral in relation to both Olympian and earthly systems; he is by nature free to indulge in both without that fear of exhaustion which is deadly to mortals. While Dom Juan, tracked by a whole group of avengers moving at an ever-accelerating pace, begins to require the shelter of various physical and verbal disguises in Acts IV and V, seeking to eliminate the other's knowledge of him by circulating incognito, Jupiter's power as ultimate "Cognoscere" frees him entirely of the innately human need for cover, for clear and meaningful signs, whether true or false. It would be a mistake to read him as an intelligent Tartuffe or a divine Dom Juan, although such analogies may be useful to us simply for our own purposes of coherence and continuity. He truly possesses the unique power secretly coveted by an avidly sought after by certain of his predecessors in Molière's theater. Jupiter can *re*-produce *origin*ality; that is, he can, like Dom Juan, enact a hybrid discourse which is self-contradictory because of the values inherent in any human system of signs, but without fear of either retaliation from his enemies or the demise of truth and meaning. He can thus safely bypass "meaningful" exchange, as Tartuffe vainly wished to do, and realize Arnolphe's impossible dream in a wholesale appropriation of women, speech, and language.[7]

Regardless of the fact that, in Molière's work, divine liberty smacks suspiciously of caste libertinage,[8] and however irrevocably Jupiter's marvels clutter the path to his goal — at times even rendering him a somewhat ridiculously helpless lover (I. iii) — he does possess that semiotic authority and aptitude specifically denied all of the other characters under consideration: the capacity to re-present meaning as meaningless presence.

For the duration of Jupiter's and Mercury's earthly visit, then, the very concept of personal identity as the responsible origin of speech and discourse is irrelevant. Amphitryon and Sosie both are and are not responsible for verbal and physical exchanges enunciated or enacted in their names by doubles whose identities both do and do not correspond to those presumably private labels. Until someone can articulate that ambiguity — that is, until Act III, scene x — Sosie, this play's "downtrodden expert in theater,"[9] remains in an impossible situation vis-à-vis everyone, a situation typified by the exchange in Act II, scene i, around which my commentary on the reconciliation of real illusions and illusory reality is centered. In order to resolve the conflict for himself, Sosie has simply floated the "je" (". . . *j'étais venu, je* vous jure, / Avant que *je* ne fusse arrivé"), judiciously allowing it to drift between Mercury and himself. His solution accords perfectly with what has "really" transpired, but because it also requires the willing suspension of belief in identifiable being, and thus of judgment and the very meaning of signs, it remains totally unacceptable for just about anyone but him. The fundamental, if impossible, proposition of this play, enunciated by Mercury in the prologue and used as my epigraph, can be summarized as the interchangeability or *reversibility* of things and words, of being and being represented. Things do not only change names according to who orders them and his respective place in an ideological hierarchy; names also switch ontological hooks — the thingness, identity, or being which differentiates them from one another, and whose separate individuality is in turn assured by names, according to the same principle. Mercury has changed names, robbing Sosie of his — or at least forcing him to stop using it. (If Sosie could in fact cooperate by dropping his name-identity, he, like Sganarelle vis-à-vis Dom Juan, would place himself in a position to compete with the gods.)[10] But Mercury has also altered his own being, equivocating both the ontological judgment fundamental to the truth or falsehood of verbal propositions — and conversely, or, in this play's terms, by the same token — that orderable state of being which lends truth-value to judgments.

Having agreed under duress to abstain from his own role whenever necessary, but fully aware of his continued and continuous presence on stage, Sosie instinctively opts for a common (non)sense, hokus-pokus solution. Significantly, that solution is reminiscent in its folk logic of Sganarelle's "moine bourru" —

certified demonstrations of morally appropriate [i.e. *safe*] behavior. Naturally, such fitting, functional anomalies appear to be simply inadmissible to Amphitryon, whose efforts to establish a reasonable alternative to Sosie's version of recent events indicate and manifest the reigning confusion. In his mounting fury he successively suggests four forms of alienated or marginal discourse that are acceptable to him as possible typologies or classifications in which to order Sosie's preposterous tale: dream, drunkenness, madness, and malicious prevarication. Each of these states of mind — fantasy, inebriation, alienation, and ill intent — implies a more or less responsible source of discourse more "symbolic," "metaphorical," or deliberately falsified than "literal" or "factual." The two former types of discourse spontaneously equivocate messages and meaning, and must therefore be read as poetry rather than as readily decodable information indicative of the real world and practicable therein.

In each case, some form of rhetorical cloudiness is implicated, be it willful or inevitable (in contrast to the preceding three plays, and especially to *Tartuffe*, the distinction carries no weight here, where *everyone* appears denuded of his or her will by Jupiter's presence in the cast), and that opacity becomes inseparable from Sosie's unmoored "I."[11] Just as in the early stages of her love-inspired apprenticeship in signs, context, and exchange, Agnès understood by direct reference to a specific code rather than through interpretation according to variable collective and individual contexts (the poetic convention common to a group and / or her particular relationship with Horace), so, by a peculiar contortion of that same process of "acculturation," Amphitryon the literalist must either encounter someone capable of articulating the present noncontext or remain in painful conflict about the meaning of Alcmène's words. Faced with the necessity of relinquishing a common adherence to constant personal identity and to collectively established contexts as constitutive of meaning that is appropriate to the semiotic data his senses are beginning to compile, the hero, renowned for his power of the sword, is reduced to humiliating impotence, whether in dialogue with his servant or with his wife.

Like Arnolphe, Amphitryon sets foot on totally unfamiliar terrain upon returning home, and, like Arnolphe, must there suffer the deprivation of his theatrical powers, of speech itself. He must ineluctably submit to that other hero gifted with control over the *Sēmē*, with the ultimate will to order and chaos. Enrique and Oronte, the genuine sources of Horace's and Agnès's power of the "I," determine the fulfillment or frustration of Arnolphe's need to possess, according to their absence or presence on stage. Similarly, Amphitryon's status as unique proprietor of his own identity, and consequently of Alcmène's desire, depends upon Jupiter's absence or presence on earth. Since the latter, unlike Enrique and Oronte, or Louis XIV's representative and the Statue, plays a principal role from the moment the curtain rises, Amphitryon never stands the slightest chance of defending his uniquely "legitimate" (that is, justifiable according to the theo-, socio-, or semiological dictates governing any one of the three preceding plays) aspirations vis-à-vis responsibility, Alcmène, or his own desire. This work is set in the context, and according to the roles, of an alienation of context effected for the express purpose of satisfying arbitrary, boundless desire, and Amphitryon's efforts to *disqualify* Sosie's narrative by defining it as marginal or alienated appear all the more comic.

By the same token, Sosie alone, like Sganarelle, possesses a truth of which his master has need, yet will not seriously consider when he clumsily attempts to articulate it, but in the end his fortune appears to be the reverse of Sganarelle's. Rather than having been cheated, he alone retains the power of speech after Jupiter's final declaration. True, he uses it only to advise silence, and thus brings about the end of the play and everyone's ability to speak. However, since the secret meaning of this work is meaninglessness (as long as Jupiter remains on stage), Sosie's revelation of silence, along with Jupiter's departure, paradoxically restores order and meaning to the universe.

The question remains as to precisely what constitutes the overwhelming power of Jupiter's stage presence upon the "I," on the responsible initiator / origin of speech and discourse. How can we read Sosie's "moi" speech in relation to Amphitryon's humiliating predicament and to the other three plays?

> Faut-il le répéter vingt fois de même sorte?
> Moi, vous dis-je, ce moi plus robuste que moi,
> Ce moi qui s'est de force emparé de la porte,
> Ce moi qui le seul moi veut être,
> Ce *moi* de *moi-même* jaloux,
> Ce moi vaillant, dont le courroux
> Au moi poltron s'est fait connaître,

Enfin ce moi qui suis chez nous,
Ce moi qui s'est montré mon maître,
Ce moi qui m'a roué de coups. [II. i. 810–20; my italics]

Mercury can hardly exercise that faculty for the deprivation of speech and identity which is unique to Jupiter, and by virtue of which Amphitryon flounders dumbly through repeated efforts to maintain some semblance of the *self-possessed* quality obligatory for aristocrats. Jupiter alone controls that decorum for lack of which Mercury finds himself strongly rebuked in the Prologue, when Night finds that his "discourse" — he is sitting on a cloud, exhausted — does not itself sit very well with his identity as a god. At that time he replies that he has no power to alter the context of his gesture, with an equivocation concerning Jupiter and the poet to which I shall return, for at this point it is still difficult to read except as a quip about poets made by a poet in a poem, another mirror-to-mirror game with representation (lines 5–46; cf. below, p. 200).

In any case Mercury *has* succeeded in strong-arming Sosie into dislocating his own discourse so that it no longer functions; even grammatically, it cannot get beyond its impossible subject. Abounding in disjunctive subject and object pronouns, it lacks a single verb. Indeed, what would be the sense of attributing a subject to a (same) subject? By garbling his syntax, Mercury effectively isolates Sosie from every other character in the play, particularly from those who presumably know him best, Amphitryon and Cléanthis. His problem lies not in his own disorientation: he has already demonstrated a penchant and faculty for repetition and role-doubling in his famous rehearsal-within-a-play scene (lines 205–59) while carrying the news of Amphitryon's victorious return to Alcmène. His extraordinary talent and versatility as an actor deliver him from the terror experienced by less practiced performers when faced with the rapid withdrawal of that name by which they defined their presence and speech on stage. Sosie knows that he still exists, that he has hardly been driven into the wings. There must be some role in store for him, and if scene i, Act I, is any indication, he will most likely adapt to it fairly easily. The principal difficulty that blocks his ability to enter into any interchange of signs lies in the equivocation of self he has experienced and cannot articulate. Everyone else refuses to accept a Sosie "poltron-vaillant" as one and the same two different people, for if they do, how can they be certain of their own status as "other" relative to Sosie? Just as Tartuffe's incognito invasion of alien systems of signs endangered an entire linguistic community, so Sosie's "moi," adrift between identity and difference, undermines each self loyal to its lifelong residence in a single port of call.

Sosie's speech is remarkably logical and consistent: each time he prefaces a "moi" with the demonstrative "ce," he clearly means Mercury, the other "moi" over there at the house. All the remaining uses of "moi" equal the "moi-même" of line 814, the self here and now relating the story to Amphitryon. His exasperated opening line thus seems understandable in that he has taken considerable care to safeguard the difference which alone will constitute proof of his presence of mind to his master. However, the necessity of employing the same name or label to his differentiated categories inevitably disorders the formal orderliness of his speech. In fact, Sosie cannot avoid delivering the message inherent in his speech (and particularly important for the art of theater): "there is [we are] an order-free order, necessarily defined, recognizable beings not necessarily immediately recognizable, nor single in our individuality. I *am* the real ['même'] Sosie, but so is another, identical to and different from me."[12] As Mercury's presence announced Jupiter's arrival, so this speech warns the reader or audience that *Amphitryon*, as a privileged real event, different from reality, draws the spectator into a twilight zone of fact and fancy, a "noncontext" wherein two mutually exclusive semiologies of meaning collide (Mercury-Sosie) at the same time that they coincide (Jupiter-Amphitryon) for the faithful (Alcmène — to her spouse and to the Port-Royal version of signification). The two semiologies coexist for a time only by virtue of the temporary effacement of the less powerful of the two, whether sensibly feigned for purposes of personal safety, as in Sosie's case, or unwittingly suffered and hopelessly resisted, as in Amphitryon's.

Jupiter's unique privilege as an aristocrat among plebes can thus be described as the freedom to switch semiotic contexts (systems or "languages," in the broadest sense of those terms) without regard for the limited modes of exchange behavior permitted by collective accord within a system of signs, for the varieties of speech that remain meaningful within a given language. Unlike Dom Juan, he can, as it were, speak a Sicilian dialect constructed of Castilian syntagms with total impunity. Furthermore, Jupiter is a god; therefore, once he leaves Mount

Olympus, he truly can create new systems or languages — "Hispanoitalian" — although they mean absolutely nothing to men, to those contributing the various signs and significant units of which they are composed. Inaccessible to his interlocutors, the significance of his semiotic behavior nevertheless qualifies it as a true language rather than a dialect, or even an idiolect, which would have to be read as variant processes (speeches) within a system. Such are the results of imposing an ontological hierarchy designed by men upon their equally human theory of signs.

Thus, in spite of fluctuations in my own vocabulary, according to the point of view or character I am positing as the (fictitious) origin of my discourse, strictly speaking, Dom Juan's use of signs constitutes an idiolect (the *process* of an attempted escape from context, system, and language), while Jupiter's qualifies as the radical creation of a new system, in spite of the fact that, unlike any other, it is not subject to the determination of a community or an appointed agency thereof. It is only a non-context in Amphitryon's eyes, and cannot be so judged once one understands the rules governing the exchange of signs in this play. Amphitryon exhibits one inevitable reaction to Jupiter's behavior: like many of the characters in *Dom Juan*, he is analogous to the Sicilian who persists in understanding a foreign interlocutor via similar-sounding phonemes, grammar, and syntax which he believes are familiar to him because of their resemblance to the semiotic units he habitually exchanges with compatriots.

Jupiter, by introducing an alien (Olympian) syntax into Theban Greek (i.e. seventeenth-century French) a syntax that can be traced entirely to his multifarious subject, creates a humano-divine system of signs, the rules or process of which remain accessible only to himself and to Mercury, who is its servant and not a participant. Elected to carry messages, he is by definition excluded from their meaning until such a time as Jupiter abdicates and men trangress the boundary between Thebes and the slopes of Mount Olympus. For the moment unchallenged, Jupiter retains the title of champion sender and receiver, for his is the largest private collection of acts, speeches, and norms relevant to the system he created and which provides his sustenance.[13] Gods and goddesses habitually engage in the kind of intercourse (speech and / or sexuality) made possible by Jupiter's presence on stage in *Amphitryon*, but in all of Greek mythology no one can rival either the constancy of

Jupiter's desire or his subsequent proliferation of signs, speeches, languages, and hybrid offspring. However, unlike Tartuffe's hybrid signs, Jupiter's offspring constitute their own genuine separate rubric of truth, a third species of being clearly distinguishable from two others in a hierarchy of signs reproduced in this play by the roles assigned to Jupiter (Hercules)[14] and Amphitryon.

Thus the paradoxical channel of communication opened up between the apex and the base of that semio-ideological hierarchy: Sosie's "floating 'I' " solution to Mercury's bodily persuasion and to Amphitryon's demand for a logical explanation partakes of Jupiter's multiform subject (man, bull, serpent, swan) as his means of satisfying an ever-present desire to escape the imprisonment of high office, to step out of the impressive dominion to which poets have mercilessly relegated him (cf. lines 84–100). Sosie remains severely handicapped in his faculty for discourse — in his agility with regard to the various individual processes practicable within the larger "language," the rules of which he has either implicitly or explicitly acquired from other inhabitants of Greece (France). According to the same principle, his desire is necessarily confined within rather narrow boundaries (Mercury elects abstinent solitude rather than share Cléanthis's bed), largely because he lacks any authoritative physical or verbal presence vis-à-vis his master, a deficiency common to servants in Molière's theater, but regularly contradicted by the creation of extraordinary exceptions like Dorine.

We recall, however, that on one level, Amphitryon mirrors a process akin to the "theater games" currently employed to train actors and actresses in the efficient adaptation and utilization of the self in rapidly alternating roles, and especially in that role to which he or she most recently played opposite. That is, *Amphitryon* is concerned with the complex act of theater. The opacity of the mask having failed, by virtue of that clumsy, artless quality which inevitably separates it from convincing representations of representation (the former being the mask, the latter the role or ersatz self it designates), and since in any case, masks, easily ripped off or fallen away, often leave the actor denuded, by what miracle can a clearly identifiable human being effect that rarefication of the self (as well as the concurrent exploitation of those real, personal qualities appropriate to his role), that transparent opacity, necessary to render his tale temporarily believable? Considering not only Molière's works *in toto* but those characters most prone to mask-wearing as well as their fate and function

within each play, it becomes apparent that, as a combined signifier / signified, the mask either no longer is, or should no longer
be, operative as a process capable of both drawing upon and en-
riching the system "theater." It remains a point of conjecture as
to the exclusive truth-value of reasons explaining or ordering Molière's reiteration of his working preference for words over masks
for the task of making possible and creating theatrical discourse.[15]
However, in *Amphitryon* that preference does relate to a general
concern with two difficult moments of transition, of which an
unworkable facilitation is thematized in *Dom Juan*. Those moments include (1) the (active) "entering *into*" / (passive) "submission *unto*," and (2) the exit *out of* the world of theater on
the part of actors and spectators alike.

Alcmène simply refuses the passage, for both her personal
integrity and her success in the unfamiliar role of spouse and
homemaker are at stake. She is therefore willing to consider only
*what is*, the perceivable fact of the matter. To an even greater
extent than Amphitryon, she remains preoccupied with being,
absorbed in her own and other peoples' judgments, attributions,
and definitions, whence her total absence from the final scenes of
the play. She never at any point involves herself with answers
provided by gods, with man's acceptance of and / or submission
to those answers, or with possible recourse to irony (i.e. meaning
not easily pinpointed, as in Sosie's closing speech), even in the
face of discourse issuing from an irrational, irresponsible, yet ultimate authority. It is rather Amphitryon and Mercury who express
concern with moments of passage,[16] while those same moments
are simply *enacted* by Jupiter and Sosie.

In fact, Sosie finds himself forced into considerable inven-
tiveness in providing the means to survive in this verbal universe,
given his base social status and consequently limited value as an
inter- and exchangeable sign relative to others participating in
and exemplifying the hierarchical social system, code, and language from which he can never permanently escape. His talent
nevertheless partakes of Jupiter's creative (re)invention of roles
designed to help him tolerate the restrictions of grandeur, as
Mercury points out (lines 80–83). Ultimately — that is, at the
opposite extremes of a social or semiological hierarchy — reprieve
lies only in release from the self, from one's own thoughts, words,
costume, face, temperament, and gestures. Sosie's semiotic relationship to the real world of things, his ability to clearly indicate,
and Jupiter's seemingly infinite puissance as Sign, Creator, In-

dicator, participant, and disruptive force in that same world, are made possible (and tolerable) thanks to the multiplicity of identities available to an exceptionally gifted performer, to that actor who reproduces an identity so perfectly that — and such is the illusory theatrical miracle wrought in and by *Amphitryon* — for a moment, representation evanesces into transparency, leaving us with a clear view of presence and origin, however unimpressive they may seem. Like an ideal medium between thought and experience, between the will to or desire for something and the act of realizing that desire, Jupiter's "I" virtually evaporates, while Sosie's becomes difficult to follow, as demonstrated by Amphitryon's angry reaction to his nonetheless syntactically logical "moi" speech.

In the cast of characters, Molière designates one role as "Jupiter, sous la forme d'Amphitryon," clearly implying that the role should be played by a character named "Jupiter." However, given the emphasis of Jupiter's need in Act I, scene iii, to articulate a husband / lover opposition (or perhaps duality), Alcmène persists in treating his role as one and the same as Amphitryon's, which is to in fact eliminate it. She categorically refuses to recognize Jupiter as "himself," ruler of the "real" Heaven and earth, as well as their most talented man of theater: "moi et moi-même," as Sosie says of the encounter between his two identical, opposite selves. The unanchored "I," and the resultingly irresponsible discourse issuing from subjects adrift in an ocean generally content to behave according to the apprehendable laws of nature, aims at the juxaposition of presence (personal identity) and representation (role-playing or the obligation to refrain from it), at the same time that it poses the question of what, if anything, such a juxtaposition might mean per se, in relation to other languages and discourse, to actors, spectators and readers, and even "out there" in the world of being. Jupiter is truly the god, king, or father who is generally absent from Molière's stage until it becomes apparent that, without him, the play cannot end, nor can order be restored. However, he is also an *actor*, an on-stage representative and staged representation of that impossible-to-play authority in the wings.

Author, origin, infinite will, unlimited desire, omniscient, omnipresent, and impossible to know or locate, Jupiter thus wanders out of bed onto the stage and asks us to believe that he is Meaning incognito.[17] Once the powerful effect of his presence relative to the other characters' behavior has been appropriately emphasized, it is essential to delineate the proportions of that influence, beginning with the enormous guffaw implicit in the very creation of such a role. Can we really take seriously the fearful charm at the disposal of this infinite libido? Can Molière fail to evoke our laughter with this preposterous character whom others designate simply as "Jupiter," while his own actions and final diatribe — along with Amphitryon's cooperative reaction to them — suggest an unabbreviated version of his name: "He-without-whom-signs-speech-language-and-order-could-not-fuction"? Doubtless, spectators and readers have rightfully understood his role as merely one more example of comic representation. Whether an actor or a speech claims to represent that very Presence whose absence necessitates representation, or an insatiably lecherous Greek patriarch, is of no great importance. Every audience, every consumer of signs, assumes that neither discourse nor personal identity can, or even should, attain that state of purportedly ideal transparancy which alone would enable representation to transcend itself. If art and reality, words and things, roles and lives, or simply representation and being "had the power to flawlessly coincide," Molière's Jupiter would not be very funny. His supposedly impossible "for real" quality would constitute betrayal, and spectators might prove incapable of outdistancing him upon leaving the theater; yet a voice in the audience might first object, "But we *invent* you precisely because you don't exist. How dare you silence us with your pretentious realization of our dream?" In 1668 such a hypothetical Jupiter would have been in danger of some type of crucifixion — a solution that would have become necessary in order for writers and painters to resume their leisurely pastime, "salons" their purposeful chatter, Versailles its judiciously planned festivals, the King his logically tautological government by decree,[18] and people such clothing as is conducive to protection from, or vulnerability to, the other's discourse.

It is thus evident that Molière created Jupiter "for laughs," for himself and for an audience in search of entertaining reinforcement. Be that as it may, we as an audience to some extent "other" need not continue recreating him *just* for laughs. Jupiter's preposterousness also reads like a pioneering experiment in representation and meaning. An a priori characterization of problems currently of fundamental interest in any articulation of a generalized science of signs, it also provides some delineation of such a science's relationship to the literary text and what we now term "hermeneutical tradition."

Inseparable from a culture permeated with that ambiguous Truth-obsessed theory of signs reiterated throughout the Port-Royal *Grammar* and *Logic*, Molière's Jupiter always, and once again, brings to light the troublesome ambiguity of the signified, or that part of the sign which provides an acoustic concept or mental image of the thing, person, or idea designated, vis-à-vis its real world referent against which to "verify" the "accuracy" of our mental image and the sign itself. In the context of rationalist thought, it is crucial to avoid any necessary correlation between our perception of something and its being, *with the singular dual exception of the self and God*, whose existence(s) is (are) demonstrated by that very power of mental representation. The clear distinction between mental and physical perception is deliberately blurred in *Amphitryon* by the very act of bringing God on stage to enact proof of his power to cast doubt on the meaning of words by equivocating the existence of the self as people define it. The plot takes place between perceptualizations of the only human perceptions verifiable by the very fact of the human's ability to conceive of them and to represent that mental representation in logical discourse.

Thus it is not humanity's perception of the world that is in question in this play, but the act of treating people as signs in need of correlation with a reality exterior to themselves, of the incorporation of being, in order to validate their existences. In addition, their God is represented as uniquely capable and desirous of casting doubt on their perceptions of themselves, each other, and Himself — that is, on their power of representation as ontological proof of the represented's existence.

In the *Meditations* Descartes begins by treating his power to think and to use language as proof of his own existence, then defines his power to conceive of a Being transcending representation (that is a Being who is unknowable to him) as proof that his indubitable self's certain capacity for representation is a result of that Presence in the universe which transcends perception and therefore must exist. In *Amphitryon*, Jupiter uses language to equivocate language (i.e. personal identity as a sign, a condition, and an origin of the meaning of an exchange of verbal signs), but never the existence of anything or anyone. Only his own existence in the eyes of mortals remains contingent upon the self he assumes. However, he also acts like an ontological control over that language, which, according to Descartes, is a fact as well as a potential for representation. While Descartes uses language to rehabilitate being, Jupiter uses being (his own presence) to debilitate the function of language, but *he can do so only if he confuses the two categories* by successfully representing himself as someone else. In fact, he has no power whatever over being or over the fact of the self, but does have an extraordinary ability to influence people's perception of being and fact. He scrambles definitions in the same way Sosie both retains and sets free the name others use to designate him, but unlike Sosie, he attempts to assimilate that talent to the power of original definition by posing as the exterior referent of which the self has no need, even when functioning as sign. A double rather than an origin, Jupiter is both a god and an extraordinary fraud.

Having established the presumed necessity of guaranteeing an ontological status to signs as both a premise of seventeenth-century linguistics and an interested stratagem on the part of one of Molière's characters, I wish to recall the inclusion of theological propositions currently under debate in the 1683 edition of the Port-Royal *Logic*.[19] If we were to first elaborate a reading of Descartes by confusing his physics and metaphysics — which is not difficult to achieve if the discourse of methodical doubt, the *cogito*, and the ontological proof are interpreted synonymously — and then infuse it with the Christian doctrine of Transubstantiation represented via Jansenism, plus an abundance of mischief à la Molière, we would end with a dubious conglomeration of predistorted discourse. That resultant blur might represent a continuing dialogue between Molière's *Amphitryon* and contemporary sign theory.

Thus, in an attempt to typify that dialogue, I have variously designated the mysteriously internalized exterior referent guaranteeing truth-value to signs as Truth, the Logos, God, Reason, or the *Sēmē*. The first four appellations can be found throughout religious, scientific, and literary texts of the period. The last is a recently revived tool of linguistics and semiology in general.[20] In my reading of the forces to which Dom Juan finally succumbs, I invoked the term "*Sēmē*" purposefully torn half-way loose from its etymology (to which Foucault and Derrida remain largely faithful) in order to relocate it astride the periphery of its historical context. The capitalization encumbers its value as sign with all sorts of anachronistic exegetical drapery not unrelated to the complex significance of the Commander's incongruous Roman garb. However, in so cloaking it in deliberate mystification, as a synonym for the various contemporary designations of the center of our systemized universe — or the zenith of desire on any one of our doctrinal hierarchies[21] — I have engaged it, by the very nugacity of its disguise, in the mischievous but well-marked detours frequently encountered in Molière's festive version of the meaning game. In most cases, the detour simply provides a bypass around the soberly diligent quality often evidenced by the numerous single-minded factual or didactic texts also produced in Molière's cultural situation. In my own case, it leads from the elaborately vague concept of a "Sēmē" to a readily accessible, although hardly univocal, attribution — *sēmantikos* ("significant"), the verb from the same root meaning "to signify, show by a sign, indicate, mean."

The detour and ambiguous concept suggest a "Molièrified Port-Royalization" of the designation "sign." However, such a model for assembling discourse from the more or less normative raw material supplied by any system or language implies the following process: a complex body of discourse whose purpose it is to represent the theory of verbal representation suggested in the plot and principal monologues of *Tartuffe*, and carefully misrepresented in *Amphitryon*, is simply superimposed upon a second text, this one relating in chronological order the complete adventures of a given morpheme throughout its historical development. Inevitably, both lose much of their separate intelligibility in the process. The innumerable traces, upon all of which depends the respective integrity of either discursive image — an integrity likely to heavily influence the accurate determination of its total representative value — intermingle individually in such a way as to cancel out one another's relationship to a formerly significant whole. Like an early Cubist scandal, the resultant mumbo-jumbo of context-deprived signs, once valorized, has the power to cause a breakdown in the current theory of representation.

First and foremost, it problematizes the a priori practicability of defining language as a vehicle for the expression of the natural order "thought," and consequently it calls into question the functional interdependence of certain cultural values: logic as the articulation of a linear progression, each step of which remains universally deducible from the one before; significance; the near-transparent quality of ideal discourse; personal identity;

the coherence of the collectivity, truth, infinite being, and behavior according to the dictates of a verifiability principle; knowledge as an appropriate ontological attribution; and, finally, power
as freedom from normative controls exerted over desire. With the
hierarchy shattered, those same values remain operative, but
without guaranteed association, that is, in ever-changing contexts
and with unpredictable results. Faced with such an irresponsible
hodgepodge of time-honored signs and asked to view it as anything other than a frivolous jest, the reader or viewer who is
faithful to the Port-Royal doctrine could only inquire, "But
what does it *mean?*" Appreciable solely in terms of the unique
syntax of its assembled lines, colors, textures, and free-floating
forms, the chaotic image, once generalized, nullifies her or his
criteria for making aesthetic judgments. If one is to *make sense*
of such an image, one must call into question the dictates of the
*Gramm*ar and the *Logic* and reconsider the laws of exchange
regulating the continuous revitalization of culture.

The notion of a "Sēmē" is thus an entirely slanted twentieth-century analogue for the classical logos, unfeasible in seventeenth-century grammar or logic, yet admissible within the group
of semiological norms comprising *Amphitryon*. Its inclusion in
this discussion as an unqualified synonym for "Logos" would
constitute as much a danger to the coherence of the whole thesis
as Arnolphe's, Tartuffe's, and Dom Juan's behavior represent a
criminal lack of responsibility vis-à-vis the rest of the cast, or the
plays read as didactic, vis-à-vis society in general. It can only claim
identical prerogatives in the same way as Dom Juan competes for
indulgence in those prerogatives reserved only for God. A culture
which adheres to the belief that the illegitimate carries meaninglessness within it, and vice versa, requires that any word born
of an assembly process expressly prohibited by the rules of the
language into which it would gain admittance be drowned in
silence. In addition, since it is not backed by a guarantee of truth
certified by higher ontological authority, its exchange value is nil.

According to all of these very same interlocking standards
(cultural ideology, political philosophy, Christian doctrine, grammar, logic), Jupiter's role should constitute a threat to the rightful order in and by virtue of which the other characters exist, as
well as to the meaning of the play, *were it not denied existence
by Alcmène, then paradoxically drowned in silence by Sosie*. The
analogy sometimes drawn between Jupiter's seduction of Alcmène
and Louis XIV's affair with Mme de Montespan thus seems ir-

relevant in terms of the semiology of meaning suggested by the play. Even if a king takes up acting as a hobby, he can only *be* himself. Whether invested by God or men, the women he favors respond to him as himself, or as himself representing someone else, regardless of the positive or negative nature of their reaction. As far as mortals can tell, Jupiter, on the other hand, retains the power to be himself and someone else at a given time, thus ensuring his success with women, whatever their persuasion. However, it is precisely because their desire bears no relevance to him as *he* knows himself, that, in suiting their own taste, they partially deprive him of gratification. As Jupiter, he stands about as much chance of securing Alcmène's love as would the King of Macedonia or Sosie.

Omniscient and omnipresent, his power to disrupt the order of words, to speak a language the meaning of which is meaninglessness, seems infinite at first glance. Sosie's accurately senseless account of chaos reigning (II. i) and his own purely voluntary departure from the stage are evidence of that power, for Jupiter cannot be reduced to silence like other Molière mavericks. Yet neither is his pompous final speech (lines 1890–1926) — this one meaningful to mortals — particularly conclusive. Present as someone else but speaking Jupiter's language, his ability to control the exchange of signs cannot be rivaled. Present as Jupiter speaking a mortal tongue according to its own rules, he finds himself heckled by the riff-raff in the audience (*Sosie:* "Le seigneur Jupiter sait dorer la pilule" [line 1913]). No one seems to care about Hercules, for ultimately people decide among themselves what it all means anyway. Indeed, if Sosie's final lines sincerely indicate speechless awe and a humble tribute to the Hercules-to-be and knowledge beyond the power of human words and understanding, then why does Jupiter's proclamation,

> Les paroles de Jupiter
> Sont des arrêts des destinées. [III. x. 1925–26]

not leave him dumbstruck? In effect, he declares that it's just fine for another superhuman hero to enter the world:

> Et chez nous il doit naître un fils d'un très-grand cœur:
> Tout cela va le mieux du monde [1938–39]

but that we should all go home and forget about it, because actually, it is entirely irrelevant. Amphitryon, to whom each line meant so much because of its potential to affirm or negate his rightful possession of Alcmène, learns that from beginning to end, he could not be cuckolded by the most powerful of gods. It is true that Alcmène will give birth to an exceptional child, but given the attitude in which Molière freezes her, dropping her role from the play soon afterward and thus eliminating the possibility of changing her mind, Hercules can only be Amphitryon's son as far as she is concerned.

Sosie's conclusion thus points out that in this purely verbal universe it is best simply to acquiesce, in their presence, to the desires of those powerful enough to disrupt meaning and continue as before once they have left. In Molière's version of the story the disruption would seem no more than a temporary halt in the eternal unfolding of discourse, an entertaining moment of necessary respite from the eminently human task of creating discourse capable of representing this orderly world and its inhabitants as the latter perceive and understand both, including the act of carrying out the appointed task.

It is thus that Molière's Jupiter is a contradiction in terms, both a god and a fraud. On the one hand, faithful to seventeenth-century sign theory, he identifies first and foremost with his name, reducing his other "selves" to purely formal nonessential disguises in which he can fool all of the people all of the time and never himself. He enjoys his escapade with Alcmène, but suffers with a name as "other" to him as it would be to everyone else, were his impersonation less perfect. On the other hand, he acts patently unfaithful to his name and ontological status, unless we redefine both "Jupiter" and "god," switching being and representation around in a manner most illegitimate according to the rules of the same theory of signs. He remains a helpless victim of the name by which he is known, just as Mercury has to collapse periodically on a cloud. The latter's gesture *is* entirely unworthy of his name and context, for gods should not have to succumb to physical exhaustion. Be that as it may, when purely a function of human language, while participating in a poem written by a mortal, he can profit only from those attributes accorded him by the poet's pen. In fact, he complains quite explicitly about having to suffer like any mortal, simply because Molière failed to supply him with a magic chariot like Night's or the tireless wings of a deity (lines 24–38). Both Jupiter and Mercury *are* the language *representing* them — that is, illogical, meaningless figments of Molière's imagination. They are truly the gods by whose names the poet calls them, even if that remains inconceivable, given their very entrapment in words representing nothing. As Sosie points out, this account of Jupiter's affair with Alcmène just *is*; like a fantasy, it does not mean anything more than the entertainment it provides.

Yet there is more. It would hardly seem appropriate to conclude a semiotic reading of *Amphitryon* by simply stating Sosie's retrospective illumination. While he does provide commentary on preceding events, his entire role, closing speech included, also constitutes an integral part of the play's meaning. The text does not end until *he* allows silence to reign, reinstating the order of representation represented in place of the disorder created by a representation of presence. It seems curious, especially if this play, and Jupiter in particular, mean nothing, that a downtrodden character representing a metaphysical order of infinitely less ontological value should restore in a single gesture the larger order shattered by temporary obligatory services unwittingly rendered to another character representing the category of being itself.

The fact is that in this work, human order cannot result from truth perceived, for, synonymous with desire, its identity transcends mortal powers of recognition. Only in his own context could Jupiter effectively wield his power of the floating "I." There he could obligate the other to fulfill his desire by abdicating his or her own will and identity, for gods and goddesses often recognize the highest of deities within an adopted form inferior to his own, and fear his wrath. They chose to obey out of fear, but not out of that dread of nonbeing inherent in a grammatical obsession with the copula or in the permanent binding together of the collective notion(s) "self-evident definition," "logical proposition," and "meaning." Gods are characterized chiefly by knowledge and will that are adequate to their desire, and tremble before Jupiter because their freedom is relative to his alone. He retains the unique power to inflict punishment in the form of frustrated desire.

Thus in terms of seventeenth-century epistemology only a god's power would be sufficient for him to submit to a god's desire. Only Olympians read divine disguise comprehensively; only they can comprehend multiple selves as also a unique knowable identity, or infinite transformation as that and single form, or change as definition, things as themselves and signs, presence as discourse, and the world as both being and language.

Mortals, on the other hand, are prone to dying, whether they are people or literary characters. It is beyond Amphitryon's, Alcmène's, or Sosie's human capability to acknowledge submission to Jupiter — even if they understood the events of the story and the nature of its characters. They could not afford to articulate submission, lest their power as and of signs — that is, their literary existence — be negated. Divested of that power in Jupiter's known presence, they recover it in his absence with the single exception of Sosie. The truth of mortals, the significance of life as limited, results only from the continual reinvention of meaning, which necessitates its essential absence if the world is to seem at all ordered to humans. It is only through the representation of representation that truth can be made "self-evident." If it is to mean anything to mortals, it must result from an unending rebirth, from an on-going process of discursive re-creation, both in the sense of work and of play. Signs and representation rehabilitate the meaning of the world, rather than the contrary; they *provide* that guarantee which the *Grammar*, *Logic*, and certain aspects of Cartesian philosophy assume must be appropriated for it elsewhere. This crucial "elsewhere" thus becomes a "here," an internalization of the "real thing" in order to validate a sign or system of signs and render it meaningful. Signs are thus treated like ideas, and representation as though it were or should be the science of logic; meaning is defined as truth which is verifiable by some perceivable or self-evident fact; and language in general is construed as a group of metaphysical categories, the essential one of which cannot be allowed to remain absent.

Amphitryon must eliminate his doubts and suspicions concerning Alcmène, not in order to create a scientific method, nor to prove that infinite being exists and that his version of the world agrees with it on a hierarchy of truths, but because he loves her. He needs no ontological scale to weigh the degree of certainty with which he can state the truth of his perception of Alcmène, but does need certain words and gestures from her, and especially, Jupiter's absence.

Molière's *Amphitryon* is thus both a meaningless fantasy, and a serious "true" statement. It *is*, and by its very existence demonstrates the patent inadequacy of the Port-Royal doctrine, for what Sosie ironically annihilates in meaningful silence at the end of the play is its negation of his own power to create meaning (lines 740–50; cf. above, pp. 169–70). The dialectic between events occurring while Jupiter is present on stage and the moral

124

delivered by the lowest man on the epistemological totem pole indicates and manifests an interpellation concerning the meaningfulness of invoking metaphysical categories to describe the language of theater.

# Semiology and Meaning
# in Classical Theater

> A *language* is . . . language minus speech: it is
> at the same time a social institution and a system of
> values. As a social institution, it is by no means an
> act . . . the individual cannot by himself either create
> or modify it; it is essentially a collective contract . . .
> the sign is like a coin which has the value of a cer-
> tain amount of goods . . . but also has value in rela-
> tion to other coins, in a greater or lesser degree.
>
> In contrast to language ["langue"] . . . speech
> ["parole"] is essentially an individual act of selection
> and actualization . . . the "combination thanks to
> which the speaking subject can use the code of the
> language with a view to expressing his personal
> thought" (this extended speech could be called dis-
> course).
>
> — Roland Barthes[1]

*Sign, Speech, and System.* Whether knowingly or unwittingly,
Arnolphe, Tartuffe, Orgon, Dom Juan, Jupiter, and Sosie all
enunciate some form of discourse that must be read (1) in the
context of a collectively contracted system of signs (values) and
the exchange thereof,[2] and (2) as deviant both in relation to that
collectivity and to the late seventeenth-century notion of an order
of things and words as absolute as it is ambiguous. If we wish
to postulate a semiology of meaning in relation to the dramatic
texts in and from which they speak to us, it remains particularly
useful to adopt the following as a working principle:

> The combinative aspect of speech is . . . of capital im-
> portance, for it implies that speech is constituted by the
> recurrence of identical signs: it is because signs are
> repeated in successive discourses and within one and the
> same discourse (although they are combined in accord-

ance with the infinite diversity of various people's speech)
that each sign becomes an element of the language; and
it is because speech is essentially a combinative activity
that it corresponds to an individual act and not to a pure
creation.[3]

On the other hand, or rather by the same token, we must not
fail to take into account the "intentionality" of the discourse in
question. As Jacques Guicharnaud aptly remarks: "La comédie
molièresque n'est ni polémique ou confession personnelle dia-
loguée, ni pur jeu d'esthète dégagé. Elle est révélation qui fait
coup double: elle vise à la définition simultanée d'elle-même et
de la réalité."[4] Viewed retrospectively, that is from the standpoint of the critical text, the "aim" of which Guicharnaud speaks
seems clear and even appears to facilitate subsequent readings of
the plays (as, for example, this work constitutes a rereading in
relation to J. D. Hubert's text or that of W. G. Moore). Although we have no indication beyond our own interpretive powers that Molière *intended* his plays to simultaneously define
theatrical discourse and the world beyond the stage, the notion of
an "aim" nevertheless retains considerable elucidative value in
view of the very process Barthes describes. Activating and ac-
tualizing speech within a given culture or system of signs presupposes a goal, that of producing "readable" discourse, or speech
which opens up possibilities of sequel. If Molière's works were
pure creation rather than an individual act of combination and
repetition within a collective contract, they would preclude interpretation in the same way that Jupiter's behavior eliminated the
possibility of meaning when seen through Amphitryon's eyes
rather than Sosie's. Similarly, a semiotic reading that would contribute to a generalized semiology of meaning in classical theater
necessitates the prior existence of both a system (Saussure's and
Barthes' principles of linguistics and semiology) and discourse
compatible with that system (e.g. Guicharnaud's text).

*Punctuating Discourse and Language.* In a political altercation
with his son-in-law, Archie Bunker, the extraordinarily popular
televised proponent and perpetrator of a certain American idio-
dialect, once commented: "You're taking it out of contest."[5]
Indicative and exemplary to the extreme of the interplay between
individual behavior and cultural norm, speech and system,
Bunker's remarks often point up problems of interpretation

within a culture and a system of signs so ambiguous that its meaning multiplies to a point of questionable intelligibility in the eyes of fellow participants in that culture. Like his hopeless puns and malapropisms, each of the highly charged signs — "repetition," "sign," "identity," "discourse," "act," "creation," "itself," and "reality" — define and enact a *coup double*, the context / contest of interpretation. To ignore either context — that is, the language within and without which an individual pieces together his or her speech — or the accompanying contest (its ideological implications), which together found the semiology of a given text, would be to falsify the insight of our own reading by vitiating its dual relationship to the text and to the self as listener and speaker. Surely the unrivaled magnitude of Archie Bunker's viewing audience can in part be traced to his eminently ambiguous yet never confusing insights into the representativeness of the self and of verbal representation *it-self*. When he complains to his spouse, "I come home and tell you one o' the great antidotes of all times, an item of real human interest, and you sit there like you're in a comma,"[6] he is not only pointing out his reaction to the discouraging passivity manifested by his audience. His listener effectively punctuates his (deviant) speech with a collectively contracted language of gesture, both supporting and undermining him. She coauthors his story at the same time that she brings it to a halt (with a pause), thus rewriting it in accordance with the very normative code for and of which — not unlike Dom Juan, albeit in a seemingly antithetical cultural context — he is attempting to provide the antidote / anecdote. The "real human interest" of discourse and, a fortiori, of discourse on literary discourse resides in just such a contest between anecdote and antidote. Without it, there can be no semiology of meaning, whether in seventeenth- or twentieth-century terms, whether in classical or modern critical rhetoric. As was the case in those moments of victory accorded to Dom Juan's antidote for poisonous contracts, meaning at that point would cancel itself out in an on-going process of irony.

Contest is thus a requisite, though not a necessarily sufficient, condition for the existence of any system of signs — symbols, indices, and signals included — and of the significant exchange of values within or in reaction to that system. It represents the bond that in the seventeenth century wedded systems of signs, ideology, and culture to a collective agreement that *there is meaning*, that a speech can be perceived as understandable, a text as legible.

Insofar as Molière is concerned, I have both established the interchangeability of the terms "meaning" and "order" and suggested an interpellation of that common accord in the case of *Amphitryon*. Thus we may restate the contract to read that *there is order*, that each of the plays discussed rests on that almost immutable principle and that its plot is set in motion by a threat posed to the existing order in the form of some variety of semiological deviance. Unlike the loudly acclaimed modern hero Archie Bunker, the Molière character who departs from a semiotic norm does not admit of contest, at least not on a permanent basis. Arnolphe, Tartuffe, Orgon, Dom Juan, and Jupiter, each for his own reasons and in varying degrees of ignorance about signs, all aim for the absolute triumph of their respective perversions. Once attained, their goals would clearly effect the annihilation of an intricate web of contractual values and, consequently, of semiotic exchange itself — except for Sosie's ambiguous gloss on Jupiter's equally equivocal intervention in the world of signs and representation.

Arnolphe might have sequestered Agnès; Orgon succeeded in helping Tartuffe cuckold, impoverish, and incriminate him and his family; Dom Juan succeeded in pursuing a happily transient existence, and Sosie, in proving that two mortals can occupy the same personal identity were it not for the timely intervention of some collectively created and supported guardian of "Order," and that order in a larger sense than whatever version of the same notion is presented within the plot (Father, Monarch, Logos, Ius, Author). Yet while Amphitryon experiences considerable difficulty in adjusting to a reversion to the world of mysterious resemblances and baffling illusions, Sosie's irony, followed by his invocation of silence, both qualifies Jupiter's behavior as entertaining but meaningless and makes sense of it in relation to the Port-Royal texts and to certain linguistic and cultural norms. That Hercules should have been born of Jupiter and Alcmène's "trompe-l'œil" union strikes us as altogether as ironic as Sosie's final tribute to the former's magnanimity.

Regardless of the author's own convictions, the culture and ideology reflected or refracted in his works both prescribes and questions faith in one God and in a unique Moment (the genesis of history) for the creation of order out of chaos, of language out of babel. The Logos alone could have initiated and remains capable of modifying the differentiation between difference and sameness. However, when that ultimate *principle* made sacred by absence finally appears on stage, we find it personified by something of a buffoon, lacking even Horace's charm with women, at least in its own name. As powerless to seduce Alcmène as Aristophanes' Dionysus of the *Frogs* is incontinent, Molière's Jupiter partakes of a long tradition of irreverent farce, on the one hand, and of the Port-Royal reverence in regard to being, on the other. If the American comic hero Archie Bunker would have his wife Edith punctuate his discourse with a comma and never pause for breath, Molière's Sosie — played by the author — would have Jupiter punctuate *L'Ecole des femmes*, *Tartuffe*, and *Dom Juan* with a question mark, even as he abjures interrogation.

*Meaning.* There is a growing tendency in contemporary literature and literary criticism to view discourse as language that has become autonomous with respect to things, as at once its own speech and system, obedient only unto itself and a minimal number of rules regarding the phonetics, grammar, and vocabulary established by languages — Spanish, German, Chinese, and so on. Manifest in Renaissance epistemology, or that theory of knowledge which is based on affinities, as well as to a remarkable degree in the works of Rabelais, the power of wielding the word as though it were a world of its own, always true in its liberated right, has once again come to the fore. Temporarily confined to poetry by the dictates of Cartesian rationalism and linguistics, words seek at once to free themselves from and dominate things, to both invent reality and encroach upon it. Whatever its "punctuation," Molière's text respects the boundary between stage and orchestra and between the theater and the real world. Late twentieth-century drama, on the other hand, pours barely distinguishable actors and spectators out into the street, though often in the name of a political ideal described as "revolutionary" (i.e. in an effort to undermine existing linguistic, semiotic and cultural norms). Everyone is free to be Jupiter, and Jupiter is free to do anything, all in the public domain. A summary of this contemporary attitude would read: "The meaning of meaning is meaning." There is widespread faith in the indestructible inward or immanent quality of signs and discourse, a faith sometimes characterized by a kind of summary annihilation-by-occupation of any exterior referent or transcendent quality. This attitude toward — if not realization of — the meaning of discourse permeates behavior with respect to all types of signs, whether linguistic or nonlinguistic.

In contrast to such an all-encompassing desire for self-sufficient speech, the semiology of meaning inherent in Molière's texts might bear the subtitle, "The meaning of meaning is meaning and Meant." *Amphitryon* doubtless postulates a signifier duly bound to its signified, yet liberated from an ever absent, continually reincorporated exterior referent of higher ontological rank than the sign itself. However, while Sosie's final lines may gloss the play, *Amphitryon* must not be considered a retrospective illumination of Molière's theater *in toto*. Even though plagued by meanings set adrift, the designation "Meant" retains its initial upper case, continuing to exist side by side with a free-floating, "equivocal" significance which it cannot erase, or vice versa. Clearly, Arnolphe and Tartuffe are foiled by that collective Order they sought to transgress and subvert for personal gain, or rather by its collectively determined representatives, by other words and other characters. Dom Juan, whom we described as a modern or Renaissance hero rather than a classical stereotype, also meets up with Order. The Statue, however, twice appears on stage before issuing its presumably ultimate summons and, in any case, who is it? Whom or what does it represent? Finally, Sosie, the blue-collar worker of seventeenth-century France, demonstrates considerably more wisdom in regard to signs, discourse, and meaning than his somewhat idiotic employer, more than even the "chef de troupe" and general director of the gods himself.

Be that as it may, we must not forget that in 1671 Molière also produced and directed the semiologically complex *Les Femmes savantes*, nor that his theatrical discourse continued to flow throughout 1672. The meaning and / or "Meant" of each play flashes clearly enough before characters and audience alike just as the curtain begins to fall. But a generalized semiology of meaning with respect to Molière's theater, and a fortiori of classical drama as a whole, awaits the careful consideration of other plays and other moments of conclusion.

# Notes

## Introduction

1. Jean-Baptiste (abbé) Du Bos, *Réflexions critiques sur la poésie et sur la peinture* (Paris, 1740), vol. I, pp. 435–46.

2. See Julia Kristeva, "Le Geste: Pratique ou communication?", in her *Recherches pour une sémanalyse* (Paris: Le Seuil [Tel Quel], 1969), pp. 90–112.

3. Gilbert Norwood, *Greek Comedy* (New York: Hill and Wang, 1963), p. 13.

4. René Jasinski, *Molière* (Paris: Hatier, 1969), p. 17.

5. Jacques Derrida, *De La Grammatologie* (Paris: Editions de Minuit, 1967), pp. 50–53.

6. Ferdinand de Saussure, *Cours de linguistique générale*, critical edition by Rudolf Engler (Weisbaden: Otto Harrassowitz, 1967), p. 26.

7. Ibid.

8. See below, Chap. 4. Molière's *Dom Juan,* in all its atypicality, remains a remarkable example of precisely that "à cheval" notion of the human potential for the exchange of signs and of the effect of its disunity in a specific social context and a specific period.

9. Saussure, *Cours de linguistique,* p. 26.

10. Noam Chomsky, *Cartesian Linguistics: A Chapter in the History of Rationalist Thought* (New York: Harper and Row, 1966), p. 2.

11. Ibid., p. 76.

12. The distinction speech / language here corresponds to the one Saussure makes throughout the *Cours de linguistique générale* between "parole" and "langue" (cf. below, the opening pages of Chap. 6).

## Chapter 1

1. René Descartes, *Œuvres et lettres,* presented by André Bridoux (Paris: Gallimard, [Pléiade], 1953), p. 1320. Unless otherwise specified, all quotations from Descartes' works and letters are from this edition.

2. Claude Lancelot and Antoine Arnauld, *La Grammaire générale et raisonnée de Port-Royal* [1660] (Menston, Eng.: The Scolar Press, 1967), p. 27. Unless otherwise noted, all quotations from the *Grammaire* are taken from this edition.

3. Michel Foucault, *L'Ordre du discours* (Paris: Gallimard, 1971), p. 12.

4. In this chapter I shall be referring to Descartes' texts specifically, and most often to the *Meditations,* as a changing and evolving metaphysics of Being and man not reducible to any series of objective truths and certainly not describable via the scientific method Descartes himself created. On the other hand, I shall also be referring to "rationalist" or "Cartesian" philosophy, and even to "Cartesian linguistics," in the second half of the 17th century. By these I mean a body of objective ideas completely separated from the ebb and flow of thought which, at the outset, in Descartes' texts, gave them their meaning. See the "Note sur le cartésianisme au XVII⁰ siécle" at the end of Ferdinand Alquié's *Descartes, l'homme et l'œuvre* (Paris: Hatier-Boivin, 1956).

5. See Alfred Simon, "The Elementary Rites of Molière's Comedy," in Jacques Guicharnaud, ed., *Molière: A Collection of Critical Essays* (Englewood Cliffs, N.J.: Prentice-Hall, 1964).

6. "Toute la philosophie est comme un arbre dont les racines sont la métaphysique, le tronc est la physique et les branches qui sortent de ce tronc sont toutes les autres sciences, qui se réduisent à trois principales, à savoir la médecine, la mécanique et la morale" (Alquié, *Descartes,* p. 5).

7. Méditation III, p. 286.

8. Ibid.

9. Ibid., p. 294.

10. Ibid., p. 295.

11. Ibid., p. 1320.

12. This assertion in no way excludes the equally important influence of Pascal's remarks on language. (See Jan Miel's very pertinent article "Pascal, Port-Royal and Cartesian Linguistics," *Journal of the History of Ideas* 30, no. 2 [April–June 1969]: 261–71.) My present concern lies with certain rationalist assumptions common to Descartes, Arnold, Nicole, Lancelot, and many other thinkers of the second half of the 17th century; those assumptions constitute part of a theory of knowledge reflected and / or represented in the language and themes of certain Molière plays. I feel that that concern and this study are both incomplete without equal consideration of the scattered commentary on language in *De l'Esprit géométrique* and the *Pensées.* It would certainly be interesting and useful to do a companion study to this one in such a light. In this chapter, however, I am focusing on a very specific relationship, that of the Cartesian criterion for "true language" — whether or not it accurately conveys the structure and content of thought — to the text of *L'Ecole des femmes.*

13. I refer to the thesis, mentioned in my Introduction, that comedy did in fact originate with beast-mummeries. W. G. Moore, in his article "Speech" (in Guicharnaud, ed., *Molière*, pp. 40–49), points out the eternal inadequacy of words to emotions which provides much of the comedy of this scene. Harpagon's exaggerated gestures accentuate the prelinguistic, animal-like state in which he finds himself.

14. *Œuvres complétes de Molière*, ed. Robert Jouanny (Paris: Garnier, 1962), vol. I, p. 472. Unless otherwise specified, all quotations from Molière's plays are from this edition.

15. This is one of the many instances in Molière's theater when semiology of meaning and semiology of communication overlap. Thus I will often allude to costuming, sets, and gesture as "signs of signs," or "signs of objects" (see Petr Bogatryrev, "Les Signes du théâtre," *Poétique*, no. 8, 1971). Whatever Molière's personal taste, for we know that he liked green, on a symbolic level not incongruous with that preference, I emphasize Arnolphe's greenness in conjunction with his jealousy and obsessional fear of cuckoldry, i.e. as a sign of a sign. His obsession, combined with the fact of his age, makes him ridiculous and therefore comic. But he is not only ridiculous. Part of his garb is black, and this color is generally associated with the mask in Molière: power gained through a show of false sobriety or wisdom, fabricated social status (Monsieur de la Souche), or hypocrisy. The mask must, of course, be ripped off, so that if Arnolphe exits on all fours linguistically speaking, from a semiological point of view he is also all green at the conclusion of the play.

The following chart demonstrates the waxing and waning of Arnolphe's monologues:

| Act I | scene i: | 3 lines | |
| | scene iii: | 5 lines | 22 lines |
| | scene iv: | 14 lines | |
| Act II | scene i: | 15 lines | |
| | scene iv: | 12 lines | 27 lines |
| Act III | scene iii: | 36 lines | |
| | scene v: | 31 lines | 67 lines |
| Act IV | scene i: | 31 lines | |
| | scene v: | 11 lines | |
| | scene vii: | 34 lines | 80 lines |
| | scene ix: | 4 lines | |
| Act V | scene i: | 4 lines | |
| | scene ii: | 2 lines | 8 lines |
| | scene v: | 2 lines | |

16. Bernard Magné, "*L'Ecole des femmes*, ou La Conquête de la parole," *Revue des Sciences Humaines* 37, no. 145 (January–March 1972): 132. The homology and the charts are reprinted from Magné's article.

17. Méditation IV, p. 306.

18. Antoine Arnauld and P. Nicole, *La Logique de Port-Royal* (Paris: Flammarion, 1970), Introduction by Louis Marin, p. 12. This question is treated in chapter 10, Part I, of the text itself. Unless other-

wise specified, all quotations from the *Logic* are taken from this edition.

19. Méditation II, p. 286.
20. Ibid.
21. *La Grammaire de Port-Royal*, p. 28.
22. Ibid., p. 26.
23. Ibid., p. 29.
24. Chomsky, *Cartesian Linguistics*, p. 4.
25. Cf. James Dickoff and Patricia Janes's Introduction to the English edition of the Port-Royal *Logic* (New York: Bobbs-Merrill, 1964), pp. xxcii–li.
26. There is a fundamental ambiguity in both the Descartes and the Port-Royal texts. The supposed innocence of the idea depends on its simplicity, while the possibility of error in judging stems from the complexity of that process. However, conceiving an idea is by the *Grammar*'s and *Logic*'s own definitions a highly complex process in itself, for it involves both the perception of an object, substance, or mode and the formation in the mind of an image of the same. The status of the exterior referent and its relationship to the signified remains unclear; it is for this reason that I have avoided any explicit discussion of the ontological status of the sign in a "Cartesian linguistics" approach to Molière's texts, although such modern preoccupations necessarily intervene from time to time in my interpretations.
27. Cf. Jules Brody, "Don Juan and the Misanthrope, or The Esthetics of Individualism in Molière," *PMLA* 84, no. 3 (May 1969): 559–76.
28. Cf. Paul deMan, *Blindness and Insight: Essays on the Rhetoric of Contemporary Criticism* (New York: Oxford University Press, 1971), pp. 102 ff.
29. Quoted in Chomsky, *Cartesian Linguistics*, p. 4.
30. In chapter 6 of the first part of the Port-Royal *Logic* the authors set up a distinction between univocal and equivocal words, each word in the former group linked to the same general or universal idea, and each one in the latter retaining the possibility of allusion to one of several ideas. In the ensuing chapters univocal words are highly valorized for their clarity and therefore availability to an ideal discourse. Equivocal words, that is, the figures of rhetoric hidden in language, lead to "confusion," disturbing language's synchrony (because they refer to anterior judgments) and the transparent quality of discourse so desirable to the Port-Royal grammarians and logicians. Whether or not Molière was acquainted with the *Logic* when he wrote *L'Ecole des femmes* (both appeared in 1662), the thematics of his theater reflect a common concern with an appropriate attitude toward figure and embellishment of any kind. However, rather than reflect it, as he does certain elements of 17th-century linguistic theory, he satirizes pretentious rhetoric, although less through Arnolphe than Alceste in the *Misanthrope* and throughout *Les Précieuses ridicules* and *Les Femmes savantes*.
31. Part II, chap. 23, p. 75.
32. Ibid.
33. Ibid., chap. 13, p. 49.
34. Roland Donzé's commentary on the *Grammar*, in his *La*

*Grammaire générale et raisonnée de Port-Royal* (Bern: Francke, 1967), p. 33.

35. Scolar edition, p. 33.

## Chapter 2

1. Michel Foucault, *Les Mots et les choses* (Paris: Gallimard, 1966), p. 58.
2. Molière, *Œuvres complètes* (Paris: Garnier, 1962), p. 630.
3. Ibid., p. 631.
4. J. D. Hubert, "Hypocrisy as Spectacle," in his *Molière and the Comedy of Intellect* (Berkeley and Los Angeles: University of California Press, 1962), pp. 91 ff.
5. Jacques Guicharnaud, *Molière, Une Aventure théâtrale* (Paris: Gallimard, 1963), p. 165.
6. Louis Marin, Introduction to the Flammarion edition *La Logique*, p. 10.
7. Guicharnaud, *Molière*, p. 135.
8. *La Logique*, p. 63.
9. Ibid., p. 80.
10. Ibid., p. 120.
11. Ibid., p. 80.
12. Ibid.
13. Foucault, *Les Mots*, p. 72.
14. Ibid., p. 79.
15. *La Logique*, Part I, chap. 4.
16. Cf. Guicharnaud, *Molière*, p. 76: "C'est un catalogue de gestes-clés qui se substitue à la confusion de la vie."
17. Foucault, *Les Mots*, p. 65.
18. See epigraph.
19. *Œuvres et lettres*, p. 37.
20. Ibid., p. 42.
21. Cf. above, pp. 42–43. Descartes' stipulation in *Regula* VI is not unrelated in praxis to the structure and function of the portraits in *Tartuffe*.
22. Foucault, *Les Mots*, p. 69.
23. Guicharnaud, *Molière*, p. 48.
24. Ibid., p. 75.
25. Descartes, *Discours de la méthode*, in his *Œuvres et lettres*, p. 135.
26. Cf. Guicharnaud, *Molière*, p. 173.
27. Jean Baudrillard, *Le Système des objets: La Consommation des signes* (Paris: Gallimard, 1968), p. 19.
28. Cf. below, opening pages of Chap. 4. I wish to clearly differentiate the respective effects on any system of signs of *desire for desire* (Tartuffe) and *desire for autonomy* (Dom Juan). The former pertains to the monarch's jurisdiction, the latter to the Deity's.
29. See above, n. 28.

## Chapter 3

1. Baudrillard, *Le Système des objets*, p. 104.
2. Charles Sorel, "Histoire comique de Francion," in Antoine Adam, ed., *Romanciers du XVII^e siècle* (Paris: Gallimard, [Pléiade], 1948), pp. 318–19.
3. Hubert, *Molière and the Comedy of Intellect*, pp. 118–19.
4. *La Logique*, p. 50.
5. Ibid., p. 150.
6. Ibid., p. 151.
7. Cf. Marin's Introduction to *La Logique*, p. 20.
8. Cf. above, p. 41.
9. James Doolittle's reading of Dom Juan's conduct (worthy humanity = manliness) seems helpful in this respect:

> . . . for Dom Juan the excellence of humanity consists in a man's realization of his manhood by functioning fully as a man, not as an angel, not as a beast, not in passive potentiality, but in active fact. He must have the aspiration, the will, the knowledge, and the courage actively to prove himself superior to the rest of nature, as well as to whatever conventional opposition he may encounter. ("The Humanity of Molière's Dom Juan," reprinted in Guicharnaud, ed., *Molière*, p. 101; originally printed in *PMLA* 68, no. 3 [June 1953]: pp. 509–34.)

10. Ibid., p. 100.
11. Director's note in Gallimard edition of Molière's works, at the beginning of Dom Juan's long monologue in II. iv.
12. *Molière, Une Aventure théâtrale*, p. 238.
13. Cf. the complete text of Doolittle's article (see above, no. 9) for a thorough discussion of Sganarelle's willingness to equate signifiers and meaning (the tobacco speech [I. i], his adventures as a doctor [III. i], his faith in Dom Juan's conversion [V. ii]). While this bilateral division of the semiotic world into truth and lie, and the subsequent inability of some to distinguish the two domains, constitutes a fundamental element in Molière's comedy, one most explicitly treated in his *Tartuffe*, Sganarelle's confusion does not seem central to my purposes, except as a counterpoint to Dom Juan's behavior, when the latter participates in the same bilateral interpretation of things and words in order to cover himself when besieged by the consequences of his previous nihilistic gestures and by his victims' increasing awareness of his mode of existence.
14. Doolittle, in Guicharnaud, ed., *Molière*, p. 99.
15. The beggar is the only other character in the play who does not use semiotic convention (clothes, rhetoric, habitat) to set himself apart from the beasts with whom he actually coexists in the forest. His behavior thus constitutes a significant difference from Arnolphe's obsessive efforts to dominate and monopolize signs or "culture."
16. The question of the "ex machina" quality of this and of certain other Molière dénouements may very well be related to the troublesome ambiguity of the referent in 17th-century grammar. In a sense, Molière's endings neatly wrap up the events of the play in an easily accessible package of meaning (aging tyrants should not force reluctant

maidens into marriage; people who try to monopolize language or wealth are ridiculous; those who fall prey to blatant religious hypocrisy are willfully stupid; etc.). However, they also provide a retrospective illumination the truth of which is authorized by someone who did not play an explicit role (Agnès's identity is established by Enrique and Oronte; Tartuffe's criminality, by Louis XIV; Dom Juan's state of sin, by God). Thus the endings function both within and without the play's structure, displaying both an immanent and a transcendent quality in relation to it.

17. Cf. below, pp. 118–119.

## Chapter 4

1. It has also become evident that in a semiotic reading of Molière's texts, except in cases like Arnolphe's costume, Elmire's cough, and Dom Juan's gift to the Poor Man, "signal," "index," "symptom," and "symbol" — terms rigorously distinguished in communications theory — must often be included under the same rubric, "sign," thus endowing them with some of the properties of Saussurian linguistic signs. (Can we hope to escape metaphor, even "dangerous" metaphor, when dealing with systems of signs in a literary text?)

However, I have tried to maintain a distinction between signs which must be *interpreted* and those to be *decoded*, and do not wish to affirm at this point that the manifest presence of a system of signs necessarily implies communication.

2. Cf. above, pp. 44–46, for Descartes' remarks concerning sameness, difference, and illusion, and pp. 71–72 for their relevance to classical discourse in general.

3. Cf. above, n. 2.

4. An allusion to the advent of "Cartesianism" as both a scientific method and vogue in the second half of the century and to the accompanying separation of scientific discourse from poetry, fact from sensory experience, metaphysics from aesthetics, etc.

5. Charles Mauron, *Psychocritique du genre comique* (Paris: José Corti, 1970), p. 105.

6. In that reason, in Part III of the Port-Royal *Logic*, and throughout Descartes, presupposes a Heaven-authorized intuition or idea (a thing as represented by the mind to itself) and thus a fundamentally correct *conception of things* available to all men. Jupiter "rationalizes" the baroque by modifying the relationship between repetition and change, thus destroying men's ability to order their conceptions, to reason or to judge them, and even falsifies representation itself (ideas or, on that other level to which I consistently refer, theatrical art).

7. Cf. above, pp. 10–11, and the opening pages of Chap. 5, for the definition of speech and language operative throughout this work.

8. Cf. Hubert, *Molière*, p. 182. I am particularly indebted to Hubert for his notion that the structure and coherence of *Amphitryon* depend largely on the complementary principles that "Rank must . . .

prevail over all other values [in spite of the gods' propensity to become its and their own victims]" (p. 182), and that in this and certain other plays "Molière . . . requires above all the incompatibility between pleasures and institutions" (p. 185) — the latter of which I have defined as necessarily characterized by a collectively contracted system or systems of signs — along with his resulting conclusion that the downtrodden Sosie also represents a "sophisticated" (p. 187) author, representative and "represented" (i.e. "signified") of theatrical art per se. That commentary has proved invaluable to me in the difficult task of interpreting Molière's *Amphitryon* both relative to and in radical conflict with a semiology of meaning fairly consistent throughout the three plays previously discussed.

9. Hubert, p. 182.

10. Cf. above, pp. 91–92.

11. See also II. ii. Alcmène and Amphitryon have similar recourse to "vapeur" (904) and "songe" (912) in their efforts to rationalize each other's apparent alienation from truth, fact, and their own actions. Sosie, expert inventor of survival techniques for underdogs, *invokes* inebriation to excuse his (Mercury's) injurious disdain vis-à-vis Cléanthis (II. iii. 1086–1116). Usually rather ill-equipped to defend himself and the claims of his desire and will (he refers to himself as "poltron" in his encounter with Mercury), his aptitude for turning the elements of a totally disorienting and disarming situation to his own advantage is surpassed only by Jupiter's own extraordinary gift. His values concerning the possession of women faithfully reflect those of his master. However, as becomes apparent from his "Vivat Sosie" (1142), he alone retains his spouse's sexual fidelity, that is, his status as exclusively desiring and desired mate. It is precisely such an aptitude for satisfying and controlling reciprocal desire that was found lacking in Arnolphe, Horace, Tartuffe, Orgon, Dom Juan, and Sganarelle, however divergent their aspirations relative to it.

12. Cf. above, p. oo, the *absolute* quality of the contemporary concept of order. One of the results of Molière's adding Cléanthis to the traditional cast of *Amphitryon* is precisely the comic "bombshell" effect of Sosie's every encounter. His verbal touch has become ruinous to his two most important relationships (with Amphitryon and Cléanthis), both of which approach near-disaster at several points in the play. While he remains somewhat less a prisoner of context than the other mortals, he also experiences more serious handicaps when trying to articulate an event or impose his opinion. Cléanthis thus not only balances out two triangular couple structures, she also brings out the paradox of Sosie's impotent power of the truth. He can and cannot, must and must not, make up for Mercury's injurious disdain of his spouse.

13. Cf. Roland Barthes, *Elements of Semiology*, translated by Annette Lavers and Colin Smith (New York: Hill and Wang, 1968): "In the linguistic model, nothing enters the language without having been tried in speech, but conversely no speech is possible (that is, fulfills its function of communication) if it is not drawn from the "treasure" of the language."

14. Cf. below, p. 121. Since he is not included in the cast of characters, I do not consider Hercules an element of the semiology of this play *except as a missing piece*, the creation of which appears of singular disinterest to everyone. Apparently the other characters are not particularly grateful to Jupiter for his addition to a certain semiology and a certain meaning.

15. This problem may also be stated (interpreted) in terms of a maturation process undergone by individual talent and an art form in general (of farce, of "high" or "low" comedy), or in terms of the existing competition for royal favor with other authors and companies. However, as I stated in my Introduction, such critical discourse imposes unnecessarily narrow a priori limits on the as yet unexplored usefulness of a generalized science of signs for the interpretation of literary works. In any case, I have no evidence that Molière actually felt such a preference for words, or even that he did not simultaneously feel conflicting preferences among various systems of signs available for conveying meaning from the stage. When I invoke the designation "Molière," it is in reference to a total mental image, a fictitious representation entirely consequent with my reading of a text. Insofar as the semiology of meaning is concerned, my "Molière," like Molière's Sosie, is a unique multiple "moi" involved in writing that same text; he either does or does not "make sense" to others, but for me his meaning can only appear self-evident, for "Molière" is also my interpretation of a play signed with the same name. Such is the subjective, unscientific nature of invoking vocabulary for a semiology of meaning (cf. Georges Mounin, *Introduction à la Sémiologie*. Paris: Editions de Minuit, 1970); such is also nascent semiology's awareness of its own possibilities and implications.

16. Cf. above, pp. 110 and 121, Mercury's fatigue with his role in the Prologue and Night's scolding as an unintended seconding of his commentary.

17.     Défendez, chère Alcmène, aux flambeaux d'approcher.
Ils m'offrent des plaisirs en m'offrant votre vue;
Mais ils pourraient ici découvrir ma venue
Qu'il est à propos de cacher. [I. iii. 530–33]

It is as though the pages of a secret love story were in the process of unfolding, the alphabet, vocabulary, and syntax of which only Jupiter and Mercury fully understand, while the former alone can reveal its final meaning. Amphitryon wishes it read aloud to him in translation, starting from the last paragraph; Alcmène does not want to hear about it; Mercury enjoys the story line but wishes he were a better-equipped scribe; and Sosie is too preoccupied with appeasing or deflecting other people's wrathful reactions to recognize his own handwriting or the sound of his own voice.

18. As is the case of the syntactically illogical, and therefore linguistically meaningless, lesson on differentiation which Cléante very reasonably administers to a logic-deaf Orgon in Act I, scene i, of *Tartuffe*, the principal significance of a proposition or group of propositions in Molière's theater sometimes lies more in the speaker's claim to *privilege* than in the elements and processes described, or goals pre-

scribed, by the rational grammars and guides to logic circulating at that time. Since privileges assumed by feudal aristocracy were never more highly valued than in the latter half of the 17th century, at precisely that period in history when they could no longer be won or justified except by royal favor, the very definition of the notion "privilege" came to require a total absence of justifiability, and, ideally, of any rationally traceable cause whatsoever. It was describable only via such tautological propositions as "Divine right belongs to Louis, because he is monarch" (at a time when, and in a country where, monarchy was defined as a divine right). It would therefore seem entirely logical for a king to re-affirm his rightful authority by forcing his subjects to acquiesce to the legality of a wholly unjustifiable decree (such as a tax levied to finance Versailles). They will do so by the sole virtue of someone else's arbitrary good fortune in life. Privilege does or does not descend, according to an unpredictability principle also behind the deliberately unjustifiable delegation of political power in the 17th century. It remains totally subject to the bestower's unfathomable will, and usually presses the grateful receiver into the posture of a powerless suppliant. His only hope of influencing fortune is to excel in a community skilled in base flattery, to beat them at their own game, perhaps with superior talent, perhaps with an interesting variation in his method or means of competing (e.g. the court jester, the serviceably clever man of letters, or the innocuous conversationalist capable of consistently appropriate witty remarks). Like a name at birth, royal pensions, Jupiter's desire, Christian grace, or death itself, the 17th-century caste privilege took root in soil already fertilized by collective faith in and fear of the lawful authority automatically ascribable to the Unexplainable (cf. Hubert, *Molière*, pp. 181 ff., "Three Conceptions of Hercules").

19. Cf. above, pp. 71–72.

20. Cf. Barthes, *Elements of Semiology*, and esp. Derrida, *De La Grammatologie*.

21. Were Molière's characters' discourse to participate less in the hierarchical game of comedy by "equivocation," as the author calls verbal language itself in his Preface to *Tartuffe* (cf. above, the opening epigraph to Chap. 2), the designation "sēmē" would more properly indicate semiology's *analogue* for the concept "Reason" in scientific method, "Logos" in Scripture, "God" in the theologian's discourse, etc.

## Chapter 5

1. *Elements of Semiology*, p. 14.

2. As proposed in my Introduction (cf. above, p. 11 and n. 12, p. 15), the foregoing reading presupposes a distinction between speech and language corresponding to Saussure's differentiation "parole" / "langue," just as my discussion of "language" in general, in contrast to specific systems of verbal signs, corresponds to Saussure's distinction "language" / "langue" (cf. above, p. 8). It is important to note, however, that, in the passages quoted from Moore (in Guicharnaud, ed.,

*Molière,* chap. 4, "Speech") or Hubert (*Molière,* chap. 9, "The Seducer as Catalyst") neither they nor I in any sense refer to the Saussurian projection of a generalized science of signs, regardless of the fact that they employ precisely the same terms as Barthes and Saussure himself.

3. Barthes, *Semiology,* p. 15.

4. Guicharnaud, *Molière, Une Aventure théâtrale,* p. 519.

5. *The Wit and Wisdom of Archie Bunker,* Foreword by Norman Lear (New York: The Popular Library, 1971), p. 5.

6. Ibid., p. 4.

# Bibliography

Alquié, Ferdinand. *La Découverte métaphysique de l'homme chez Descartes.* Paris: Presses Universitaires de France, 1966.

———. *Descartes, l'homme et l'œuvre.* Paris: Hatier-Boivin, 1956.

Anderson, J. D. "The Language of Gesture," *Folklore* 31 (1920): 70 ff.

Arnauld, Antoine, and Pierre Nicole. *La Logique de Port-Royal.* Edited by Charles Joudain. Paris: Hachette, 1872.

———. *La Logique, ou L'Art de penser,* 1662–1683. Introduction by Louis Marin. Paris: Flammarion, 1970.

Arnavon, Jacques. *Le Don Juan de Molière.* Copenhagen: Gyldenal, 1947.

Auerbach, Erich. *Mimesis.* Translated by W. R. Trask. Princeton: Princeton University Press, 1953.

Barthes, Roland. *Elements of Semiology.* Translated by Annette Lavers and Colin Smith. New York: Hill and Wang, 1968.

———. *Essais critiques.* Paris: Le Seuil, 1964.

———. *Le Degré zéro de l'écriture, suivi de "Elements de semiologie."* Paris: Gonthier, 1971.

———. *Mythologies.* Paris: Le Seuil, 1957.

Bateson, M. C. "Kinesics and Paralanguage," *Science* 139 (1963): 200 ff.

Baudrillard, Jean. *Le Système des objets. La consommation des signes.* Paris: Gallimard, 1968.

Bayle, François. *The General System of the Cartesian Philosophy.* English translation, dated 1670.

Bénichou, Paul. *Morales du grand siècle.* Paris: Gallimard, 1948.

Benveniste, Emile. *Problèmes de linguistique générale.* Paris: Gallimard, 1966.

Birdwhistell, Ray. "Communication without Words," in "L'Aventure humaine," *Encyclopédie des sciences de l'homme,* vol. 5. Paris: De la Grange Batelière, 1968.

Bray, René. *Molière, homme de théâtre.* Paris: Mercure de France, 1954.

Brody, Jules. "Don Juan and the Misanthrope or the Esthetics of Individualism in Molière," *PMLA* #3, vol. 84 (May 1969): 559–
76.

Brosin, Henri W., ed. "Paralanguage: 25 Years after Sapir," in *Lectures
in Experimental Psychiatry* (Pittsburgh: University of Pittsburgh
Press, 1966).

Brown, Roger. *Words and Things.* Glencoe, Ill.: The Free Press, 1958.

Burke, Kenneth. *A Grammar of Motives.* New York: Prentice Hall,
1945.

———. *Language as Symbolic Action.* Berkeley and Los Angeles: University of California Press, 1968.

Busson, Henri. *La Religion des classiques.* Paris: Presses Universitaires
de France, 1948.

Camus, Albert. *Le Mythe de Sisyphe.* Paris: Gallimard, 1942.

Chomsky, Noam. *Cartesian Linguistics: A Chapter in the History of
Rationalist Thought.* New York: Harper and Row, 1966.

———. *Language and Mind.* New York: Harcout, Brace, Jovanovich,
1972.

———. *Problems of Knowledge and Freedom (The Russell Lectures).*
New York: Random House, 1971.

Colish, Marcia L. *The Mirror of Language, A Study in the Medieval
Theory of Knowledge.* New Haven: Yale University Press, 1968.

Critchley, M. "Kinesics: Gestural and Mimic Language: An Aspect of
Non-Verbal Communication," in *Problems of Dynamic Neurol-
ogy* (Jerusalem: Hebrew University Press, 1963), pp. 181–200.

———. *The Language of Gesture.* London: Arnold, 1939.

deMan, Paul. *Blindness and Insight: Essays on the Rhetoric of Contemporary Criticism.* New York: Oxford University Press, 1971.

Derrida, Jacques. *De La Grammatologie.* Paris: Editions de Minuit,
1967.

———. *L'Ecriture et la différence.* Paris: Le Seuil, 1967.

———. *La Voix et le phénomène.* Paris: Presses Universitaires de
France, 1967.

Descartes, Rene. *Œuvres et lettres.* Presented by André Bridoux. Paris:
Gallimard (Pléiade), 1953.

Descotes, Maurice. *Les Grands Rôles du théâtre de Molière.* Paris:
Presses Universitaires de France, 1960.

Doolittle, James. "The Humanity of Molière's *Dom Juan*," *PMLA* 68
(June 1953): pp. 509–525.

Du Bos, Abbé Jean-Baptiste. *Réflexions critiques sur la poésie et sur la
peinture*, vol. 1. Paris, 1740.

Ducrot, Oswald, et al. *Qu'est-ce que le structuralisme?* Paris: Le Seuil,
1968.

Ehrmann, Jacques. "Notes sur *L'Ecole des Femmes*," *Revue des Sciences Humaines* 109 (January–March 1963): 5–10.

Fernandez, Ramon. "Molière," in André Gide, ed., *Tableau de la littérature française de Corneille à Chénier.* Paris: Gallimard, 1939.

———. *La Vié de Molière.* Paris: Gallimard, 1930.

Foucault, Michel. *Folie et déraison: Histoire de la folie à l'age classique.*
Paris: Plon, 1961.

———. *Les Mots et les choses.* Paris: Gallimard, 1966.

————. L'Ordre du discours. Paris: Gallimard, 1971.

"From Stage to Street," Yale French Studies 46 (1971).

Gossen, Emmett J., Jr. "Les Femmes savantes, métaphore et mouvement dramatique," The French Review 45 (October 1971): 37–45.

Gossman, Lionel. Men and Masks, A Study of Molière. Baltimore: The Johns Hopkins Press, 1963.

Gouhier, Henri. L'Essence du théâtre. Paris: Plon, 1943.

Greimas, A. J. Du Sens, Essais sémiotiques. Paris: Le Seuil, 1970.

Gueroult, M. Descartes selon l'ordre des raisons. Paris: Aubier, 1953.

————. Nouvelles Réflexions sur la preuve ontologique de Descartes. Paris: Vrin, 1955.

Guicharnaud, Jacques, Molière, Une Aventure théâtrale. Paris: Gallimard, 1963.

————, ed. Molière: A Collection of Critical Essays. Englewood Cliffs, N.J.: Prentice Hall, 1964.

Hall, Gaston. Molière: Tartuffe. London: Edward Arnold, 1960.

Handke, Peter. "My Foot My Tutor, a play," TDR/The Drama Review 15 (1972): 62 ff.

————. "Nauseated by Language," TDR/The Drama Review 15 (1972): 57 ff.

Hayes, Francis. "Gestures: A Working Bibliography," Southern Folklore Quarterly 21 (December 1957): 218–317.

Hjelmslev, L. Essais linguistiques. Copenhagen: Nordisk Sprog-og Kulturforlag, 1959.

Hubert, J. D. Molière and the Comedy of Intellect. Berkeley and Los Angeles: University of California Press, 1962.

Jakobson, Roman. Essais de linguistique générale. Paris: Editions de Minuit, 1963.

Jasinski, René. Molière. Paris: Hatier, 1969.

————. Molière et Le Misanthrope. Paris: Colin, 1951.

Kristeva, Julia. Recherches pour une sémanalyse. Paris: Le Seuil, 1969.

Lamy, B. De L'Art de parler. Paris, 1676.

Lancelot, Claude, and Antoine Arnauld. Grammaire générale et raisonnée (1660). Menston, Eng.: The Scolar Press, 1967.

————. La Grammaire générale et raisonnée de Port-Royal. Edited by Roland Donzé. Bern: A. Francke. 1967.

————. La Grammaire générale et raissonnée de Port-Royal. Introduction by Michel Foucault. Paris: Paulet, 1969.

Ledoux, Fernand. Molière, Le Tartuffe. Paris: Le Seuil, 1953.

Leroi-Gourhan, A. Le Geste et la parole. Paris: Albin Michel, 1964–65.

Magné, Bernard. "L'Ecole des Femmes, ou La Conquête de la parole," Revue des Sciences Humaines (January–March 1972): 137 ff.

Martinet, André. Eléments de linguistique générale. Paris: A. Colin, 1960.

————. A Functional View of Language. Oxford: Clarendon Press, 1962.

————. Le Langage. Paris: Gallimard, 1968.

————. La Linguistique synchronique, études et recherches. Paris: Presses Universitaires de France, 1970.

Mauron, Charles. Des Métaphores obsédantes au mythe personnel, Introduction à la psychocritique. Paris: José Corti, 1963.

————. Psychocritique du genre comique. Paris: José Corti, 1970.

Michaut, Gustave. *La Jeunesse de Molière. Les Débuts de Molière à Paris. Les Luttes de Molière.* Paris: Hachette, 1922–25.

Miel, Jan. "Pascal, Port-Royal, and Cartesian Linguistics," *Journal of the History of Ideas* 30, no. 2 (April–June 1969): 261–71.

Molière [Jean-Baptiste Poquelin]. *Œuvres complétes.* Edited by Robert Jouanny. Paris: Garnier, 1962.

Moore, W. G. *Molière, A New Criticism.* Oxford: Clarendon Press, 1949.

Mounin, Georges. *Introduction à la sémiologie.* Paris: Editions de Minuit, 1970.

Norwood, Gilbert. *Greek Comedy.* New York: Hill and Wang, 1963.

Peirce, Charles Sanders. *Philosophical Writings of Peirce.* Edited by Justus Buchler. New York: Dover, 1955.

Plato. *The Timaeus.* Translated and edited by Francis M. Cornford, under complete title of *Plato's Cosmology, The Timaeus of Plato.* London: Routledge and Kegan Paul, 1956.

Romano, Danilo. *Essai sur le comique de Molière.* Bern: A. Francke, 1950.

Romanowski, Sylvia. "L'Illusion chez Descartes: Thèmes et structure jusqu'aux Méditations." Ph.D. diss., Yale University, 1970.

Sapir, Edward. *The Selected Writings of Edward Sapir.* Berkeley and Los Angeles: University of California Press, 1949.

de Saussure, Ferdinand. *Cours de linguistique générale.* Critical edition by Rudolf Engler. Weisbaden: Otto Harrassowitz, 1967.

———. *Cours de linguistique générale.* Paris: Payot, 1972.

Sauvage, Micheline. *Le Cas Don Juan.* Paris: Le Seuil, 1953.

Scherer, Jacques. *La Dramaturgie classique en France.* Paris: Nizet, 1950.

Sebeok, Thomas A. "Coding in the Evolution of Signaling Behavior," *Behavioral Science* 7 (1962): 430–42.

Simon, Alfred. *Molière par lui-même.* Paris: Le Seuil, 1967.

Todorov, S., et al. *Théorie de la littérature.* Paris: Le Seuil (Tel Quel), 1972.

Trager, George L. "Paralanguage: A First Approximation," *Studies in Linguistics* 13, Nos. 1 and 2 (Buffalo: University of Buffalo Press, 1958): 1–13.

Villiers, André. *Le Dom Juan de Molière, Un Problème de mise-en-scène.* Paris: "Masques," 1947.

*The Wit and Wisdom of Archie Bunker.* Forward by Norman Lear. New York: The Popular Library, 1971.